The Obstinate HORSE

and Other Stories from the China Inland Mission

The Obstinate HORSE

and Other Stories from the China Inland Mission

Devotionals by Bruce Garrison

Shoals, Indiana

The Obstinate Horse and Other Stories

PUBLISHED BY KINGSLEY PRESS
PO Box 973
Shoals, IN 47581
USA
Tel. (800) 971-7985
www.kingsleypress.com
E-mail: sales@kingsleypress.com

ISBN: 978-1-937428-18-1

Credits:
Cover illustration by Ed Ulyate
Layout and graphic design by Edward Cook

Contents

Publisher's Foreword

Recently a man who was part of the underground church in China wrote a book about his life in China, how the Chinese church was established in the past, and what it is like to be a Christian in China now. At the beginning of his book he talked about a missionary who went from Norway to China in 1901. Her name was Marie Monsen. She was an amazing person, and she did many great things for the church in China as a missionary with the China Inland Mission.

In 1999 this man from China visited Norway, and while he was there he wanted to visit the grave of Marie Monsen. In Chinese culture the memory of people who have done great things is cherished for many generations, and he wanted to remember Miss Monsen for the wonderful things she did for the church in China. He went with some Norwegian friends to the graveyard where she had been buried in 1962. To his surprise, there was no headstone on her grave; it was just an empty lot that had been untended for many years. The man from China felt that this was a terrible insult!

He asked the Christians of Norway to build a new grave and put a proper headstone on it in memory of Marie Monsen. He told them that if they didn't do it, there were Christians in China who would walk all the way to Norway to do the work themselves! Two years later in 2001 a ceremony was held, and a beautiful new headstone was unveiled in memory of Marie Monsen.

It is good to remember those Christians of the past who have done wonderful things for God and for other believers. It is important to remember the sacrifices they made for the kingdom of God. It is good to remember that God works in many different ways, and that He is still able to affect our world in ways that many would say are just not possible. It is also good to remember that God answers prayers—not just the prayers of those that we would think are the most holy, or most famous, Christians. But God answers the prayers of ordinary boys and girls, dads and moms, grandpas and grandmothers. He still stretches out His mighty hand and impacts our world.

This book is about remembering. The first story is about that same Norwegian missionary, Marie Monsen, and how God protected her when she was on a ship that was captured by pirates.

But most of all, this book is about remembering the Almighty God who still moves in our world and changes lives today. He still answers prayers when people are in danger, or hungry, or lost, or in need of the message of God's love for them.

In 1865 a man from England, named J. Hudson Taylor, felt called by God to start a missionary organisation, called the China Inland Mission, that would take the message of Jesus to every part of China. At that time, most people in China had never even heard of Jesus. Hudson Taylor believed that God is able to do great and mighty things if we trust Him and ask Him to help us in everything. Everybody in the China Inland Mission believed the same way, and God answered many of their prayers, as you will see, because the stories in this book are taken from things that happened to missionaries that were working with the CIM. They did wonderful work all over China until 1951, when the last missionaries had to leave the country because of the communist takeover.

However, that did not stop God or the missionaries. They prayed and asked God what they should do, and they began to see that many other parts of Asia were also in need of the message of Jesus. So the missionaries of the China Inland Mission began to go to many other nations. They were now known as the Overseas Missionary Fellowship. Some of the stories in this book are from the countries where they began to work. Even today they continue to work for Jesus in many countries under the name, OMF International. The people and the name may have changed, but their faith and trust in almighty God remain the same!

We hope these stories will help you remember the things God has done and the people He has used in the past. But we also hope that they will help you to see that God is still the same and that He still does amazing things in the lives of ordinary people like you and me when we trust Him enough to obey Him.

Bruce Garrison
Searchlight Publications
November, 2004

Acknowledgements

No project like this is ever the work of only one person, so it is appropriate to say thank you to several different people. First, thanks to my own children, Josiah and Bethany, for liking the original copies of these books enough to encourage us to reprint them. Thanks to Mike Barton for doing the initial typesetting, and to Edward Cook for the final design (and numerous free consultations). Special thanks to Ed Ulyate for the excellent front cover illustration. I am also grateful to my friend Graham Higgins for suggesting that we add devotional sections to each chapter, and to his mom, Julie, and my wife, Pippa, for helping me to "keep it simple." Finally, I wish to express my gratitude to Sara Foster of OMF International in England for her cooperation, encouragement, and timely suggestions during every aspect of the publishing process. All glory for any good that comes from the reprinting of this book belongs to God.

Bruce Garrison

Original Introduction

to

The Pirate Ship and Other Stories

CHILDREN enjoy true stories, especially when truth is more exciting than make-believe. The first and the last stories in this collection have appeared before, "Pirate Ship" in Miss Marie Monsen's *A Present Help* and "Pearl's Secret" by Mrs. Howard Taylor, a best seller a generation ago. Both have been suitably abridged and adapted for the child reader of today. Acknowledgement is gratefully made to Miss Agnes Clarke for "Five Loaves and Five Cucumbers," Mr. George Birch for "Mr. Chen's False Teeth," Miss Margaret Quirk for "The Rat Who Lost His Tail," Mr. and Mrs. Walter Moody for "Little Good News," Mr. Howard Hatton for "Dangerous Taxi Ride," and Miss Hanni Schäffeler for "The Rain Stopped in Time." Much of the initial work of collecting and editing these stories was done by Mrs. Jeannette Clarke. The illustrations are by Mrs. Marjorie Campbell.

Pirate Ship

YELLOW SEA JOURNEY

MARIE MONSEN looked round her "cabin" with a rueful smile. It was little bigger than a cupboard, had bare boards for a bed, no window, and was thick with dust. All the other cabins were filled, and as this one, belonging to the Mate, had been offered to her, she gladly accepted it.

"It is only for one night," she thought. She was the only white-skinned person on board, though there were several hundred Chinese passengers. Having seen her suitcases safely put in the cabin, she went out on deck to talk to her fellow-passengers and to give out leaflets which told the Gospel in a simple way for those who had never heard it. As darkness fell, she went to her cabin, knelt in prayer by her hard bed, and then lay down, fully clothed, to sleep. She felt sure that God meant her to make this journey because she had prayed much about it.

Very early next morning she was startled by the sound of pistol shots, the shrieks of passengers, doors being wrenched open, and people running up and down. Twenty pirates had mingled with the passengers and, once at sea, compelled the captain at pistol point to change course. Now the passengers were being ordered out of their cabins down to the hold.

"Oh dear," thought Marie, "How awful! Pirates!" Immediately she remembered a verse in the Bible that had often been a comfort to her in times of danger. She repeated it to herself in this way.

"Fear not, Marie, for I am with you; be not dismayed, Marie, for I am your God; I will strengthen you, Marie, yes, I will uphold you with my victorious right hand." And then she added, "Lord, I will obey and *not* be afraid."

The pirates came to her cabin one after another and ordered her down to the hold, but as they never stopped to see their orders carried out, she stayed where she was. "God gave me this cabin," she said to herself, "so here I shall stay."

A second lot of sixty pirates came aboard with guns and ammunition. They broke the lock of Marie's door and came in and out freely. Her only defence was prayer. One of the leaders held a pistol at her head, saying, "I'll shoot you!"

"No, you can't shoot me just when you like," she replied. Somehow all her fear had been taken away. "My God has said, 'No weapon that is formed against thee shall prosper.'"

Again and again in the days that followed, Marie heard him say, "Just think! She says I can't shoot her whenever I like because her God says that no weapon that is formed against her shall prosper." One man stole her wrist watch, but surprisingly, a man who seemed to have some sort of authority and was more friendly to her than any of the others ordered it to be returned to her.

On the second day Marie noticed that the cabin had fittings for an inner screen door. If only she could have that door!

There seemed to be only one of the real crew about, so when he brought her small allowance of hot drinking water she asked him if he knew where it was. "Yes," he replied, "and when the pirates are smoking their opium I will bring it up." He did so, and helped Marie to fix it in position. How wonderful it was to have some air, and yet to be able to fasten her door again on the inside!

For five days the ship, under its new command, steamed up and down, shooting at every boat that came in sight, and then capturing and looting them. Marie's cabin was situated between the pirates' headquarters on the one side and the ammunition store on the other. Day and night pandemonium reigned. After five days Marie was utterly exhausted from the noise and lack of sleep. But there was nothing to do but pray! "Lord, let me sleep. I ask You for sleep." Miraculously, the ship suddenly became quiet and Marie fell sound asleep. After the ship had anchored in a secluded estuary out of sight, it was never so noisy again.

About this time Marie's friends had heard that the ship had fallen into the hands of pirates and were praying earnestly for her. And their prayers were heard. From that time on, instead of feeling as if she were swimming against the stream, it was as if she were being borne along on a strong current to a safe landing.

After looting the passengers' clothing, the pirates paraded up and down outside Marie's cabin in fine silk garments, looking very ridiculous. For a few days they all wore spectacles too! New bicycles from the hold also provided hours of entertainment, as one after another tried to ride them up and down the narrow deck.

This deck was the place, too, where the pirates chose to have their meals consisting of all sorts of luxurious tinned foods they had stolen. They often offered some to Marie, who replied,

"No, thank you!"

"Well, tell us what you would like to eat, and we will try and get it for you."

"No, thank you! I can't eat stolen food; and whatever I asked for, you would only go and steal from other people."

"But you will die of starvation," they said.

"No, my Father in Heaven is able to keep me alive," she answered. And this is how her Heavenly Father fed Marie.

She had bought some apples the day before she sailed without really knowing why, and she had been given four boxes of chocolates. These with a few biscuits were all the food she had, so she divided it up into rations to last for nine days. The nine days had passed, the food was gone, and there was still no hope of being freed. But Marie was not worried, just interested to see how the Lord was going to supply her need now!

On the tenth morning before it was light, there was a gentle scratching on Marie's door. She had been thinking of the story of Elijah and the ravens, and as she jumped down from her bunk she said to herself, "This is the raven!" It was the Mate whom she had not seen since they sailed.

"Have you any food?" he whispered.

"No, I haven't," she truthfully replied.

"Let me come in then. The guard is on the other side of the ship. I have a box full of eggs here in my cabin and a tin of cakes. You can have them all. I bought them in Tientsin with my own honestly earned money." Saying this, he pulled out the treasure from among the buckets of paint, old shoes, empty paraffin tins, and other junk. Every day he appeared at that early hour, took four eggs, boiled them, and brought them back to her. Her daily ration became four eggs and two sweet cakes, and the supply lasted out until they were rescued. Marie was never hungry.

The weather was stormy and bitterly cold, and Marie had brought no bedding. As she was going to a warmer part of the country and expected to spend only one night at sea, she had packed all her winter clothes. But God knew what she would need and had made provision beforehand. Just before she started out, a belated Christmas parcel had arrived containing a warm cardigan and woollen stockings. The post that day had also brought no less than five fat bundles of newspapers from home. "Oh, dear," she had sighed, "why didn't these things come earlier? I shall have to take them with me now, and my baggage will be heavier." How glad she was of that warm cardigan! The newspapers came in very useful too, for, pinned inside her coat, they helped to keep her warm at nights.

The days dragged by. More than two weeks had already gone. An intense desire filled Marie's heart that the hundreds of passengers and the thirty-five members of the crew, all of them heathen, might see that hers was a living Almighty God.

Often one or other of the pirates said to her, "Don't you know you are worth a lot of money?" —showing that they hoped to get a good ransom for her. Sometimes they deliberately tried to make her impatient, usually by saying they meant to keep her captive for a long time.

"Don't you ever get impatient?" they would ask her.

"Do I look impatient?"

"No, that's just what you don't look. Whatever we do, we can't provoke you. Aren't you longing to go ashore and get away from us?"

"No, I'm not, and I thank God for that. He sent me to China to preach the Gospel, and now He wants me here to preach the Gospel to you, so I'll stay as long as God wants. It is He who has allowed this to happen."

"Can you understand such peace?" she heard them say to each other. "We can see it in her face. The other passengers look quite different. They get more and more impatient every day!"

Nearly three weeks had passed. Then government gunboats were reported to be nearby, and preparations were made to flee

17

with the loot. About fifty junks, moored alongside the ship, were loaded with food and other stolen goods. But the great question concerned Marie and what to do with her. For hours they argued, and Marie could hear all that they were saying through the thin boards which divided her cabin from their headquarters. It was clear that only the Lord could deliver her. As she prayed He reassured her with His Word in Psalm 31:20: "Thou shalt hide them in the secret of thy presence from the pride of man: thou shalt keep them secretly in a pavilion from the strife of tongues."

Plans were finally made to leave the ship at 3 pm on the twenty-first day, but Marie was so sure that God was not going to let her be carried off that she dared to tell the pirates so!

Just before the zero hour a tremendous storm arose around the ship, causing all the junks to cast off in great haste and make for the shore. When the storm subsided Marie neither heard a sound nor saw anyone for some hours. The pirates evidently believed that it was her God who had sent the storm to protect her. But the next day they decided to go ahead with their original plans. But when their spies returned, Marie could hear loud arguments and sounds of disagreement among the leaders. Then the time for their daily opium came, and nothing more could be done that day. The day following, as they were about to leave, Marie heard one of the pirates say,

"Go and tell the foreigner to get into the junk at once. We must go!" Hearing steps on the deck, Marie jumped to her feet.

"Lord, what will You do now?" she breathed.

The door was flung open and a pirate faced Marie. He stood staring for a long time, but without speaking a word; nor did he cross the threshold. Then, without delivering his message, he slammed the door and went off. Marie heard him say, "You can do what you like to me, but I can't give your order!"

That evening an unexpected chance came for Marie to talk to the pirates about Christ for two or three hours.

"We are bad, only bad," said one. "We were born bad. We do evil from morning to night, and from night to morning. You were born good. You don't hate us like the other passengers."

"Yes," they all agreed, "that is quite true." To which Marie replied that she was born with the same evil heart as they, and went on to tell them of the Saviour who came to save all men and give them new hearts. They were clearly impressed, for they listened to her in complete silence. It was an evening they would never forget.

Next day was Sunday, the twenty-third day of Marie's captivity. Just after noon the sound of distant gunfire was heard, and after much running about, most of the pirates left the ship. Those left released the Captain from his cabin and ordered him to take the ship up the estuary. But it was too late. A gunboat was hard on their heels. In the cabin next door Marie heard fragments of a conversation:

"We *must* take the foreigner with us. . . they won't dare to shoot if they see we have her. . . but how can we? She would have to run, and after eating nothing for twenty-three days, she couldn't walk, much less run." Marie thought she recognized the voice of the friendly pirate who had returned her watch.

"Hurry! Hurry! There's no time to lose," shouted someone; and with that, the last of the pirates left the ship.

Marie, her heart full of thankfulness, was soon out of her cabin. Looking out over the water, she saw some of the pirates already on shore in full flight, littering the path with discarded garments as they ran. Others were making for the shore as fast as they could in the boats.

Seeing this, Marie ran down to the hold where the passengers were imprisoned, shouting, "Come up! Come up! The pirates have all gone!" But no one stirred. Again she shouted down to them, "I am the foreigner. The pirates really have all gone. Come up and see." Cautiously they emerged and when they saw their former captors fleeing pell-mell across the sands, they forgot their usual Chinese dignity and laughed and cried and embraced one another. Then, rather sheepishly, they apologized to Marie.

"Forgive us, please. You see we have been sitting with a sword pointed at our hearts for twenty-three days!"

The original voyage southwards was now resumed without the unwelcome fellow-passengers. So Marie had four more days on that ship to witness to God's faithfulness. The other travellers said to her, "Your great God has helped you, but none of our small gods has helped us!" This was Marie's great opportunity to speak of the One who is "our refuge and strength, a very present help in trouble" and of the Saviour who can also rescue us from our sins and set us free (Psalm 46:1).

What about me?

"So do not fear, for I am with you; do not be dismayed, for I am your God. I will strengthen you and help you; I will uphold you with my righteous right hand" (Isaiah 41:10).

My world is full of many things that could cause me to be afraid. Some of them are about nations or people or even weather patterns. What do I do when I am afraid? Who do I look to for help? Do I let God be my friend and protector? How can I be sure that I am letting Him be the one who helps me in difficult times? What can I do to learn what it means to really trust God? (For further study you can read Proverbs 3:5-6.)

Heavenly Father,

Thank you for your mighty hand that reaches out and holds me when things seem to go really wrong. When I am afraid, help me to learn to trust you. Teach me to be still and wait for you to show me that you are always there to help me when I am in trouble, even when I am not always aware that you are with me. Amen.

2

Five Loaves and Five Cucumbers

AD 1900. A MISSIONARY FAMILY IN CHINA

IN a little Chinese home built round a courtyard, Vera was listening to her father reading from the Bible, "....they wandered in deserts, and in mountains, and in dens, and in caves of the earth" (Hebrews 11:38).

"What's dens and caves, Daddy?" she asked.

"They are big holes in the hillsides where wild animals sometimes live."

"Are there any near us?"

"Yes, lots."

Vera could not read yet, and of course there were words she could not understand, but she liked the sound of them.

Oh, how hot it was outside—like an oven! Drought! It

had not rained for months. Birds fell down dead from thirst and heat. Fields that should have been green with wheat were parched and cracked, with only thistles growing in them.

Among the idols in the city temple was one called "The god of rain." Priests had burned incense before it, chanting prayers for rain almost day and night, but not a drop fell.

"We'll take him out tomorrow," said the head priest, "and carry him shoulder-high all round the city to see the dried up fields. We'll let him roast and have a taste of what he is making the people suffer because he won't send rain." But even that didn't help.

The mayor of the city called a meeting of the chief men.

"There *must* be someone holding up the rain. We must find out who it is, or we shall all starve to death."

Suddenly one man spoke up. "Why, I know who it is. It is those 'Ocean People' (meaning the missionaries from across the ocean) living in our city. Get rid of them, and the rain will come."

"Right you are! Splendid idea," agreed the mayor. "I'll send some soldiers to the missionaries' home tonight. We'll drag them out of the city and kill them."

Late that night Old Chang, the mission gatekeeper, was startled by a quiet rap at his door. Peeping through a little slit in the window paper he saw a friend.

"Let me in, and don't speak loudly," whispered the man. "I've something very important to tell you."

"There are angry words being spoken in the city tonight," said the man. "The mayor blames all this lack of rain on the missionaries; they are to be taken away and killed."

"But why?" asked the gatekeeper, astonished. "Everyone knows they are good and kind, and heal many people without money."

"The mayor is too angry, and the city people too frightened to be reasonable," replied the visitor. "You must persuade them to escape *at once*. Hide them if you like, but don't tell me or anyone else where they are." And the man hurried away stealthily.

The trembling gatekeeper knocked on the missionaries' door to break the news.

"Pastor, you must all leave the city tonight! Hurry; just pack a few things and take some food, and I'll lead you to a temple in the mountains very seldom used. The keeper is a friend of mine and you can trust him."

Very quickly two or three small bundles were made up, and in soft-soled shoes the little group of five—Mr. and Mrs. Green, Miss Gregg, and the two children—followed the kind gatekeeper through a quiet part of the city, across fields, and up into the hills. Mother led Vera, Father carried two-year-old John, and Auntie Jessie looked after the bundles.

After walking for about two hours, they reached a temple high up on a cliff. The temple keeper was a kind man and felt sorry for the "Ocean people," whose reputation was good, and gave them a tiny room rather like a cage behind the huge idols.

"You will be quite safe here," he assured them. "No one has come to worship at this temple for months. But don't speak above a whisper as the hills all round here echo every sound."

Several days passed. The temple keeper gave them simple Chinese food and was very kind. Vera and John were ever so good. Sometimes the keeper escorted his five guests briefly through the temple courts for a breath of air. Suddenly one afternoon they heard someone climbing and panting. From their hiding-place the missionaries saw a young Chinese gentleman arrive and walk leisurely around the idols. Although he did not appear to have noticed them, they felt sure he had, and they were alarmed.

As soon as it was dark the temple keeper whispered in great distress,

"I can't think what made that man come here today. I don't know him, but I'm sure he saw you. He is probably a spy and will go and report to the soldiers who will come and capture you. I'm terribly sorry, but you mustn't stay here any longer. I know of a cave nearby which is almost impossible to find and I'll take you there. Follow me as quietly as you can."

Taking some food and water, the little party started down the mountain, crossed a river bed, and climbed another steep ridge. Suddenly their guide pointed to a slit in the hill a few feet away, almost hidden by grass.

"That's the cave," he said, "crawl in!" And he left them.

Wriggling in one by one, they found themselves in a huge, high, damp cave. By now all were beginning to feel ill, and the dark, chilly cave was the worst place for them. Outside it was still oven-hot. The food and water the kind temple keeper had given them did not last long. Sometimes in their thirst they sucked grass, or tried to wet their lips from drips in the rock sides.

A little book of Bible verses called *Daily Light* often comforted them, and they felt God so near to them. But the third day they were all very weak and really ill, shivering in the damp cave, and so thirsty and hungry. That morning when Auntie Jessie read in the little book, "Give us this day our daily bread," she added, "Yes, Lord, please do, and also send us something to drink to help it down !"

From the cave's low entrance they could see soldiers searching the hills for them, but evidently no one knew about this slit in the hillside. On the third night they heard footsteps approaching, and loosened stones rattling down. The moon was full. The footsteps finally stopped right outside the cave's mouth, and a man said softly in Chinese, "Is there anyone inside?" Father made the sign for absolute silence. Again the voice asked, "Is there anyone inside?" Again dead silence. For the third time the question was repeated, "Is there anyone inside this cave?"

Vera's father thought, "If we answer, this man may come in and kill us. But if we don't answer, we shall all die of hunger and thirst." So he said clearly, "Yes, please come in." And in crawled a Chinese man with a bundle under his arm. All eyes were on that bundle. Could there be food in it? Or perhaps something to drink? The man, a complete stranger, stood up, and when his eyes got used to the darkness, he counted five people in the cave. This was his story:

"This afternoon I was grinding corn on the millstone just outside the east gate of the city when a voice said to me, 'Buy five loaves (small steamed buns) and five large cucumbers.' At first I went on grinding, but the inside voice kept saying, 'Buy five loaves and five cucumbers,' until I did so. Then the voice said, 'Go where I tell you!' I took the path into the hills, turned where I felt I ought, crossed the valley, and climbed this mountain till I felt I must stop. I have never been here before, and I could not see anything like a cave where anyone might be hiding. I have brought five loaves, just made this afternoon, and five cucumbers. When you have eaten them we must leave here. I will take you to a farmer friend of mine who has a house in the next valley. He will take care of you."

How delicious those long juicy cucumbers were! Their tongues and throats were so dry and swollen that they could not have swallowed the bread alone, but slowly sucking a piece of cucumber, then taking a bite of bread, they managed to eat.

Wasn't it wonderful that this man, a stranger, and not a Christian and not knowing *why,* should buy and bring the exact number of rolls and cucumbers that God's five starving children needed?

"Now then," said the man, "if you are ready we must start. I'll carry the little girl, and let's hope no one sees us."

So once more the missionaries and the two children were escaping for their lives. Although it was broad moonlight, and they had to pass a village, no one was about, and not a dog barked to raise an alarm.

"They wandered in. . . mountains, and in dens, and in caves of the earth." Vera understood now what dens and caves were.

(An incident from missionary experience in 1900 during the Boxer Uprising.)

What about me?

"And what more shall I say? I do not have time to tell about Gideon, Barak, Samson, Jephthah, David, Samuel and the prophets, who through faith conquered kingdoms, administered justice, and gained what was promised; who shut the mouths of lions, quenched the fury of the flames, and escaped the edge of the sword; whose weakness was turned to strength; and who became powerful in battle and routed foreign armies. Women received back their dead, raised to life again. Others were tortured and refused to be released, so that they might gain a better resurrection. Some faced jeers and flogging, while still others were chained and put in prison. They were stoned; they were sawn in two; they were put to death by the sword. They went about in sheepskins and goatskins, destitute, persecuted, and ill-treated—the world was not worthy of them. They wandered in deserts and mountains, and in caves and holes in the ground" (Hebrews 11:32-38).

Throughout history many people have been ready to try great things for God. Sometimes it meant taking big chances and risking everything, even their lives. Have I ever had to risk anything for God? What has it cost me to be a Christian, a follower of Jesus? What would I be willing to give up for Jesus, or so that somebody else could find Jesus? Is there anything that I would not give up for Him? How much did He give up for me? (For further study you can read Philippians 2:5-11.)

Heavenly Father,
Over the years, you have had many followers who were willing to give up everything for you and for your work on the earth. I haven't had to do those kinds of things, but I want to be willing to

take chances for you. Give me the strength to stand strong for you at those times when being a Christian is going to cost me something. Help me remember that there are great rewards for those who choose to walk with you—no matter what. Amen.

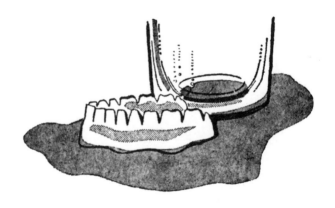

3

Mr. Chen's False Teeth

"IF you don't want the teeth, you don't have to keep them!" said Dentist Sung, angrily.

"Your bill is far too high!" equally angrily replied Mr. Chen. "You said it would be much less than the price you want now, so I'll pay you only for pulling my teeth, and you can have these back!" Pulling out his false teeth, Mr. Chen slapped them on the table in front of his nephew, Mr. Sung, the dentist.

They were sitting in a coffee shop on the main street of a town in Borneo. The fact that they were in a public building did not keep the two men from talking about their private affairs. In fact, they spoke more loudly so that people *would* hear and judge for themselves who was right and who was wrong.

For a couple of weeks Mr. Chen went without his teeth. Every time he appeared in public he felt self-conscious without them. But there was something else that made him feel more unhappy. He had been angry with his nephew in public, and he was still angry. People saw his sunken cheeks and were reminded of the quarrel.

True, everyone knew the dentist was a hard man to deal with, and that his charges were often much more than they should be. But Mr. Chen was a Christian. He really loved the Lord and could not bear to think he had disgraced his Master. But what could he do? He did not like to give in now.

Trying to explain how he felt, he said, "Before I was a Christian, I took a man to court for increasing his price like this. It was only a few *rupiahs* more than the agreed price, but I wouldn't let him get away with it. The other man wouldn't acknowledge that he was wrong until I challenged him to kill a chicken, and swear with an oath that he spoke the truth. He wouldn't go so far as that, and so I won the case."

But Mr. Chen was not winning now. By ill-feeling in his heart, he was losing to the great Enemy of the Lord he loved. He began to lose his joy in reading his Bible and did not enjoy the Sunday services.

"It's no good! I'll have to pay for those teeth," admitted Mr. Chen at last. "My nephew's price is unreasonable, but I did ask him to make them, and as a Christian I shall have to take them. But he can wait a few weeks! I'll get my son to pay him when he comes home."

But in a few days some money from Mr. Chen's son was brought to the house just as Mrs. Sung, the dentist's wife, happened to be chatting with Mrs. Chen in the kitchen.

"Now is the time for me to pay for the teeth," said Mr. Chen. "The money is here, and Mrs. Sung is here. But no! I still don't feel happy about paying."

Neither did he feel happy about not paying. He remembered he had read in the Bible, "Let not the sun go down upon your anger." Many suns had already gone down on Mr. Chen's anger, and he felt uncomfortable about it.

"I can't let the sun go down tonight without settling this matter once and for all," he thought. Then he prayed, "O Lord, help me to do what is right!"

Immediately he knew what the Lord wanted him to do. He went into the kitchen and paid over the money to Mrs. Sung. What peace and joy flowed into his heart as soon as he had done it!

Mr. Chen was soon wearing his new teeth and how splendid they looked when he smiled! Better still, everyone knew he no longer had any ill-feeling in his heart against his nephew.

What about me?

"Therefore, if you are offering your gift at the altar and there remember that your brother has something against you, leave your gift there in front of the altar. First go and be reconciled to your brother, then come and offer your gift" (Matthew 5:23-24).

Sometimes I have arguments with people. Sometimes I am wrong, and sometimes I am right. How do I treat the people I am arguing with? What can I do to stay out of arguments? How can I change my attitude? Do I always have to prove that I am right? How will anger toward another person change my relationship with God? Am I willing to say I'm sorry, even if I feel that I have been treated badly? What did Jesus do when men put Him on the cross? (For further study you can read Luke 23:32-34.)

Heavenly Father,
You are gracious and are always willing to forgive me. Help me to learn to forgive others and to do the right thing when I feel like I am being treated wrongly, or if I think I am right in my actions but others don't seem to see it. Give me the strength to stop my arguments quickly so that they don't wreck my relationships with others, or my relationship with you. Amen.

4

The Rat Who Lost His Tail

"We haven't read from this story-book for some time," said Mrs. Wang, as the young missionary settled down for her daily language lesson with her teacher. It was quite true. Usually they read from the Gospels, but occasionally they read from Chinese story-books.

"Once upon a time," the teacher read in Chinese in a sing-song voice.

"Once upon a time," the young missionary read after her, watching the Chinese characters on the page, and at the same time imitating the teacher's tone of voice.

"There lived a rat. . ."

"There lived a rat. . ."

It was the story of a rat who never could make up his mind about anything. If you said to him, "It's a fine day," he would answer, "Yes, quite fine. Oh, I don't know. Perhaps it will rain after all." If you asked him to meet you in the morning, he would say something like this: "I don't think I can manage to come in the morning, so we had better meet in the afternoon. Oh no! I shall be busy in the afternoon, so perhaps the morning would be better. But it might rain in the morning, so we'd better wait until the day after tomorrow!"

One night there was a dreadful storm—and the shaky old house where this rat lived was in danger of tumbling down. The rat-friends who lived with him woke him up and told him they must all leave the house right away. Mr. Rat wouldn't believe the house would fall down so suddenly, but a great gust of wind shook it just then, and he began to change his mind. Maybe he would leave—just in case!

Mr. Rat's friends would not wait for him to make up his mind, but went without him. Then Mr. Rat went to the doorway, wondering whether he should leave or not, and saying to himself, "What a heavy rain!" when suddenly the walls leaned in towards each other, there was a loud crash, and the house really did fall down.

Mr. Rat jumped for his life and escaped just in time, all except for his tail, which was cut off as he jumped through the crumbling doorway. After this adventure Mr. Rat learned to make up his mind quickly and not dilly-dally any more.

Now the young missionary had prayed very often for Mrs. Wang and felt sure that God was answering her prayer. But little did she know what was going on in the mind of the teacher as they read together that afternoon. Months later, Mrs. Wang told her.

"When we started reading the Bible together," she explained, "I began to feel uncomfortable, because I was sure that what we read was true. But in our home we worshipped our ancestors, and we burned incense to our household gods. Somehow, they didn't go together—Bible reading and burning of incense.

I couldn't make up my mind what to do. Sometimes I wanted to believe on the Lord Jesus. But how could I upset my parents and the rest of the family? Again and again I nearly became a Christian, but changed my mind again as I thought how upset my family would be.

"Thank the Lord," she continued, "He spoke to me through the story of the rat who lost his tail. I saw that if I hesitated too long, I should never become a Christian. So I definitely took the step of trusting Christ as my Saviour, and a few weeks later I was baptized."

What about me?

"As Jesus was walking beside the Sea of Galilee, he saw two brothers: Simon called Peter and his brother Andrew. They were casting a net into the lake, for they were fishermen. 'Come, follow me,' Jesus said, 'and I will make you fishers of men.' At once they left their nets and followed him.

"Going on from there, he saw two other brothers, James son of Zebedee and his brother John. They were in a boat with their father Zebedee, preparing the nets. Jesus called them, and immediately they left the boat and their father and followed him" (Matthew 4:18-22).

There are many things in my world that call for all my time and attention. Some of them are good things, and others are clearly bad things. Sometimes it is hard to make a choice, and even harder to make the right choice and do the right thing. When I must make up my mind to do the thing that would please God, do I find it hard to choose the right thing? If I make the right choice in my mind, how hard is it to really do the thing I know I need to do? Do I ever take the time to ask God what He wants me to do, or do I just rush to make up my own mind, without thinking about Him and His ways? What kinds of things that could turn my eyes from Jesus do I need to watch for? (For further study you can read Matthew 13:1-9, 18-23.)

Heavenly Father,
Just as when He walked on this earth, Jesus still calls people to follow Him today. Sometimes it is hard, and I am not always sure which way to go. Help me to walk with you and to keep away from all the things that could stop me from being all that you want me to be. Give me the strength to make good choices and the courage to do what I know will be pleasing to you. Amen.

5

Little Good News

A LITTLE one-roomed tribal shack on a steep hillside in North Thailand was the home of Mr. and Mrs. Noah and their little daughter, "Good News." This little girl had been God's gift to Mr. and Mrs. Noah soon after they had believed on the Lord Jesus, and she was specially precious to them, since others of their children had died.

At the simple service where they had dedicated her to the Lord, Mr. Noah said, "We are going to call her 'Good News,' because we would like God to use her to spread this message which has brought such happiness to us and such deliverance from the power of evil spirits."

But one early morning, just as the light of a new day was beginning to filter into that dark valley, in the little house on the hillside there was only fear and anxiety, for little Good News was very ill indeed. Her father was away; there were no doctors in that far-away place. Poor Mrs. Noah! What was she to do?

"I'll get Widow Sing to call the missionaries," she thought. "Hasn't the Pastor read to us more than once from God's Word, 'Is any of you ill? He should send for the elders of the church and they should pray over him.'" And so, in a short while, there was a little group gathered with the missionaries round the unconscious sick child. Very earnestly one and another prayed. After a time she seemed better and fell into a deep sleep.

The heathen neighbours gathered round too, to stare and comment, and they asked, "What are you going to sacrifice to appease the demons?"

"We do not worship demons any longer, nor do we sacrifice to them," replied Mrs. Noah. "We trust in the Lord Jesus who has delivered us from fear of evil spirits. He hears our prayers without any sacrifice of pigs or chickens."

That afternoon Mr. Noah and the other men of the village who had been working in their fields a long way from their homes returned, and little Good News had become dangerously ill again. Hour after hour the poor little body was racked with convulsions. The missionaries could do nothing; they could not even explain why God had allowed this in spite of their prayers. At last Mr. Noah said, "Shall we ask God either to make her better quickly, or to take her to be with Him forever?"

"And what will you do if God does take her?" asked the missionary.

"I will thank Him," said Mr. Noah.

The whole group approved of this, so again they prayed together. Now they felt the matter was really in the Lord's hands, and He would do what was best. Not long after that, little Good News was out of her sufferings, for God had taken her to be with Himself. Though in tears, Mr. Noah thanked the Lord for answering their prayers.

Now the neighbours crowded in, but instead of ridiculing, they stood and whispered in silent wonder as they saw how Mr. and Mrs. Noah had accepted the loss of their little daughter. There was no wailing as in the heathen homes; they had accepted God's "No" for an answer.

Before the large meal which is provided for the mourners at a burial service in those parts, there was an opportunity to tell the heathen neighbours the Good News once again, of how the Son of God loved sinful men of this world, and came to save them from their sins, and from the power of evil spirits, and of how when they died, He took those who trusted Him to be with Him forever.

Mr. and Mrs. Noah missed little "Good News" of course, but how happy they were a year or two later, when God sent them *twins* to take her place!

What about me?

"For I am convinced that neither death nor life, neither angels nor demons, neither the present nor the future, nor anything else in all creation, will be able to separate us from the love of God that is in Christ Jesus our Lord" (Romans 8:38-39).

Death is a fact of life. One day everybody has to die. Some people don't die until they are very old, but others die when they are very young. Do I know anybody that has died? What kind of feelings do I have when I think about what it means to die? Am I frightened of the parts of death that I don't understand? How does being a friend of Jesus change the way that I think about death? Do followers of Jesus ever really die? (For further study you can read John 11:25-26.)

Heavenly Father,

There are all kinds of diseases, wars, and famines in our world; and many children are dying in many different places. Sometimes it is a scary thought. But with you in my life I don't need to be afraid of death—mine or anybody else's. Teach me to know that there is nothing that can ever keep me away from you. Help me to understand that life with you means life forever. Amen.

6

Dangerous Taxi Ride

In a street bright with neon lights and noisy with blaring radios, bicycle bells, motor horns, and other traffic noises, Jee Long sat in his taxi and watched the crowds flow by— men in Western dress, women slim and graceful in their long skirts and gauzy over-blouses, Buddhist priests in their yellow robes, and beggars in their tatters. This was Bangkok.

Jee Long's mind, however, was not on the familiar scene before him. He was thinking, "What a difference it has made to my life since I became a Christian! I can take my problems to God now, and He helps me to solve them. And what a comfort my Bible is to me; so often, as I read, it seems as if God is speaking to me personally."

But his thoughts were interrupted here by a couple of men and their wives looking for a taxi. Instantly Jee Long was alert. He must get them for passengers before someone else did.

"Taxi?"

"Yes," answered one of the men. "We want to get to Lopburi tonight."

"Lopburi," thought Jee Long, "I should be able to make quite a bit out of this trip. It is nearly 100 miles."

Aloud he said, "That will be 100 *baht.*"

"Thirty," replied one of the prospective passengers.

"Ninety-five," said Jee Long. And so they bargained back and forth until both sides had agreed on a price.

In a very short while Jee Long had threaded his way through the crowded city streets on to a road lined with tall trees and jungly undergrowth. It was faintly lit by the rising moon and was empty except for an occasional small animal scurrying across the road, its eyes shining in the glare of the headlamps. Jee Long's thoughts were busy with what he would have for his supper at the end of the journey. Rice, of course. Then in his mind's eye he began to visualize the vegetable dishes he would order to go with it, fish too, perhaps, and last of all some mango with condensed milk.

Suddenly one of the men said, "At the next turning, leave the main road!" Jee Long turned round to find a gun pointing at him. His heart sank. "So they are robbers! Well, I can't argue with a gun!" There was nothing for it but to obey.

"Stop here! Get out and walk over there!"

"There," Jee Long noticed, was the edge of a steep drop into thick jungly undergrowth.

"Now turn round!"

As he obeyed Jee Long realized he was about to be shot, and his body would fall over the edge and be lost in the under-growth. He was very much afraid, and there was no one to help him. Or was there? Yes, God was there with him. So silently in his heart he prayed, "Dear God, please save me from these robbers."

Just then he heard one of the women saying, "Why shoot him? We've got the taxi and his money and other belongings. Just tie him up and let's get away quickly." So Jee Long was gagged with a dirty bit of rag and tied firmly to a tree. He heard his taxi start up and drive off, leaving him in the silence of the jungle. He tried to loosen the rope which bound him, but the harder he tried, the tighter it became.

"Have I been saved from shooting to die of starvation, or be torn by wild beasts?" thought Jee Long in horror. And then he remembered God had heard his prayer once. Perhaps He would hear him again. "O God, please help me to get free!"

Then he wriggled and pulled this way and that until suddenly something gave way, and he was free. He snatched the dirty rag from his mouth, stretched his cramped limbs, and set off to find a place to spend the rest of the night.

It was many hours before he found food and shelter but his thoughts, as he tramped wearily along the road, were full of wonder and gratitude. God *had* heard his prayers, *had* saved his life. As he thanked God he said, "This life that You have saved now belongs to You. Show me how You want me to spend it."

And God did show him. The next day the police found his taxi abandoned in the jungle, and later the thieves too were caught. At the trial Jee Long asked for a lenient sentence for the would-be murderers, to their great surprise. That experience in the jungle had brought him a new experience of God's loving care and led him to a better way of life. His taxi was sold to pay for his training as a preacher, and Jee Long is now busy telling others of a living God who hears and answers prayer.

What about me?

"'Because he loves me,' says the Lord, 'I will rescue him; I will protect him, for he acknowledges my name. He will call upon me, and I will answer him; I will be with him in trouble, I will deliver him and honour him. With long life will I satisfy him and show him my salvation'" (Psalm 91:14-16).

Sometimes things happen in life where there seems to be no hope. People get themselves into big messes where there seems to be no way out, or things around them seem to be out of their control. Have I ever been in a dangerous or difficult place that I thought was hopeless? How would I deal with it if I was? Would I even bother to call on God or trust in Him to help me? How trustworthy is Jesus in bad times where there doesn't seem to be any way out? (For further study you can read Matthew 8:23-27.)

Heavenly Father,

There are times in my life when I am afraid or confused, and everything around me seems really bad. Help me to see that with you nothing is ever hopeless. If I learn to live each day with you as my friend, I can always call to you, and you will help me even in the hardest times. Help me to see how much you care for me, and how powerful your mighty hand really is. Amen.

The Rain Stopped in Time

Rain! rain! rain! For weeks and weeks it had rained. The missionary trudging all alone along the country road in West Kalimantan (Borneo) looked at the dripping rubber trees around and thought, "Poor people! They can't do much rubber tapping in this weather, and many of them will have a hard time to make ends meet!"

Then her thoughts went ahead to the little group she was on the way to visit. Just over a year ago some new believers had started regular services, and now nearly forty attended the church.

Rubber tappers are poor people, for the most part, and depend on small clearings in the forest to grow their rice. Wages from rubber tapping provide other needs. And yet from their meagre resources this group was supporting a student at Bible School. Pressure lamps are expensive, but such a lamp was considered essential for evening meetings, when neighbours were free to come in and hear the Good News these people had to tell. So they had bought one.

In their enthusiasm the Christians had even planned to build their own church. But that had been in October before the rains started and rubber tapping had ceased. In February it was still raining, and the discouraged group badly needed the lessons from Nehemiah about prayer, trust in God, and perseverance. Now it was May, and still it was raining! That Sunday afternoon, though it was not her turn to preach, the missionary had felt she must visit this little group. One of the leaders, seeing her coming, greeted her warmly:

"Oh, Teacher, how nice to see you; we didn't expect you today! Come in and have some tea! How wet you are!"

And in reply to a query, "Yes, it has rained for months, and we haven't been able to do any rubber tapping."

With tea and chat the minutes passed. Presently the all-important subject of the church building was mentioned.

"Only today we were offered twelve good posts very cheaply, as the owner has to have some money quickly. But we have only a sixth of the amount asked in the church funds. Mr. Wen has promised to lend the rest, interest free, but we do not feel happy about the church going into debt. What do you think, Teacher?"

"Quite right," said the missionary, "but God can give you the money if you ask Him. Let's pray about it anyway."

Then she enquired, "How long do you have to raise the money?"

"Till next Sunday."

"If you had good weather and you all worked hard, how long would it take you to earn enough money?"

"Four days, perhaps."

"Well, why not promise to give the Lord what you could earn in four days and trust Him to give you four fine days?"

The Christians looked at one another in astonishment.

"This is a new idea," their looks seemed to say, "it has been raining for months, and there is no sign of it stopping yet."

But their faith was kindled, and the four or five Christians present together pledged about half the amount needed, and then they asked the Lord so simply and earnestly for enough fine weather to earn the money they had promised to give Him.

That night they invited the missionary to preach instead of the evangelist who had not been able to come. Her subject was Abraham's faith, and the congregation learned by heart the verse, "Faith gives substance to our hopes and makes us certain of realities we do not see" (Hebrews 11:1, RSV).

After the service the plan to raise money for the posts was laid before the Christians, and more earnest prayer was made. When all the money pledged was added up it was enough to buy not only the posts but a plot of land as well.

Next morning the sun was shining, but the trees were still too wet to do any rubber tapping that day. The missionary could not wait any longer and started for home.

"Don't forget the verse we learned yesterday," she called out as she said goodbye.

During the days that followed, the missionary's thoughts and prayers often turned to her friends in that little village. She heard nothing from them, however, until one day she happened to meet one of them in the street. Before asking the question on the tip of her tongue, she could see by his beaming face that her prayers and theirs had been answered.

What about me?

"Elijah was a man just like us. He prayed earnestly that it would not rain, and it did not rain on the land for three and a half years. Again he prayed, and the heavens gave rain, and the earth produced its crops" (James 5:17-18).

Throughout history people have asked God to help them in very special times. They have needed things that would usually seem impossible, and He has answered. Would I have the faith to ask God for something that looks silly to everybody else? Do I let God be in every part of my life by praying about everything that is going on around me, whether it seems big or small, possible or impossible? Do I pray about something once and then forget it, or do I trust God enough to keep asking until I have an answer? (For further study you can read 1 Kings 18:41-46.)

Heavenly Father,

The greatest gift that you have given me is that I can talk to you through prayer. You love to hear my thoughts, my needs, my dreams; but many times I forget to take the time to talk to you. Please help me to remember that you are always waiting to hear me when I call. Help me to see that you are the God of the impossible, and you care about everything in my life, even the things that I think seem small or that don't really matter. Amen.

Pearl's Secret

Sunbeams are wanted most in dreary weather, and that was just when Pearl began her shining. Her older brother and sister had to leave home and take the long journey across Siberia to Sweden. Silently her mother travelled back with Father to their home and there was Pearl awaiting them— sweetest and sunniest of babies! Her mission as a sunbeam had begun.

Pearl's father, with his colleague, was responsible for the mission hospital in Kaifeng, Honan—the only hospital in an area larger than the whole of England. From far and near the patients came. Mother's days were full with visitors curious to see the "foreigners" and with helping in the church which had been founded in the city. Five years passed, with family separation and reunions, the work of the hospital, and spreading the news of the Gospel far and wide.

The children in the doctor's home, busy though they were with games and lessons, loved to do what they could to help in the great work. Singing for Mother's friends and in the wards had always been a favourite task. They had no fear of the sick people, and many a tired face would brighten as they went from bed to bed with their sweet songs and flowers. For the wealth of the garden was theirs to use in every way they could think of to give pleasure to others. They delighted to make all the house look fresh and gay as well as to make posies for the children in the hospital or Sunday School. The three kept bravely to their self-appointed task, Pearl especially, though only six or seven years old. While the older ones were at lessons, Mother used to love to watch her little figure in its pink frock flitting among the rose bushes and to see the faithfulness with which she went about her preparations. In winter, when the flowers were gone, picture cards took their place, or a packet of sweets for each child. Then when the time came, if Mother was delayed by visitors, her little helpers would go off all the more earnestly to begin the singing and talk with the children as they gave away the gifts. No wonder the boys and girls from the crowded homes around them loved the Sunday School. Parents became interested, and one family was entirely changed through the influence of the class upon a little girl. So anxious was she never to miss, that she put down a mark every day on the wall of the living room and counted patiently till they came to seven—that was Sunday! Then she went off to the hospital and came back full of all she had heard.

Up like a lark in the morning, Pearl's days were full of radiant happiness. She was always the first to run into Mother's room to waken her with kisses, and she and her brother were soon off to the garden or to care for their pets. But first they would sit down quietly while he read their daily portion—a few verses of the Bible—the bright heads close together, as Pearl listened with keenest interest. She was keen about everything, lessons as well as play, and was so full of pluck and spirit that this brother was a companion after her own heart. To be in everything and to be "in first" was Pearl's instinct, and she wanted everybody else to be "in first" too, and to have as good a time as she had. In her perfectly childish, natural way, she wanted above all else to be good and to please God.

"How shall I please God?" she wrote on a scrap of paper one day. "If I am obedient it will please God; and if I am patient and unselfish and good, it will please God." She was thinking as she grew older, and her heart turned to the best things as a flower to the sun. "Why do I love Sunday?" she wrote in answer to Mother's question; "I love Sunday because it is unlike all other days. It is a more restful day. We have more time to read our Bibles and to pray."

Unknown to the children, a shadow was creeping over the hearts of their parents. They had long foreseen that partings must come when the three would have to leave the inland city for school life in a more bracing climate. They needed companionship with others of their own nationality, and needed to be removed from close contact with the degrading influences of heathenism. Then it was that, facing years of painful separation, the parents realized how good God had been to them as members of the China Inland Mission in preparing schools for their children, not away on the other side of the world, but comparatively near at hand so that the family circle could be reunited once in twelve months at least.

The schools at Chefoo looked out on the rocky promontory of the Bluff which encloses this beautiful harbour, with its long sweep of sandy beaches. It was early on Sunday morning when the little travellers from that far inland city arrived, and their first experience was the united service of the three schools when boys, girls, and tinies, together with teachers and parents

and visitors, joined in an hour of praise. There were two ᴄ
hundred of them, and they had nearly all come from missio.
homes and were separated from their parents, some of whoᴀ
were several months' journey away. And there was the group of
teachers, men and women who were foregoing the privilege of
direct mission work that they might give their lives to teaching
and training the children whom God had entrusted to the Mission.

How exciting that summer was to the trio and their parents—long hours on the shore, rowing, swimming, gathering
shells, and exploring the beaches! There were the exhibitions
of the three sections of the school with concerts, prize-giving,
musical drill, gym displays. There was the Sunday morning
down by the sea when a number of the boys and girls confessed
their faith in Christ by baptism. Chinese converts were baptized
as well, both men and women. East and West certainly met
under that sunny sky when schoolgirls and Chinese women,
men and boys went down into the sea and were baptized into
the one and only Saviour. To the three children, Pearl and her
sister and brother, the singing in English and Chinese of "Happy
day, happy day, when Jesus washed my sins away" as each little
group came up out of the water was a special joy.

Very quickly, as it seemed, the time came when Father and
Mother had to go back to the great city near the Yellow River,
and the three children were left, one in each of the schools. A
ray of sunshine in the parting was Pearl's joyous little face as she
went off to the "Prep" so brightly, saying,

"It's all right! I know I shall be happy."

And happy indeed she was from the first among her new-
found friends. Pearl entered heart and soul into her lessons. She
loved play too, and was never so happy as when she was helping
somebody else. No one could help being drawn to the sweet,
sunny-faced child who lived so completely out of herself and

was such good company. Everybody loved her and felt her influence for good. But perhaps it was her music teacher who knew most of the child's inner life, for on the cover of the notebook in which the gist of her music lessons was carefully recorded, the little hand had written:

"We will make it our aim to be well-pleasing unto Him."

They had counted the weeks, the days, and almost the hours, and now at last they were home for the holidays! The long journey over, first by steamer and then by train, they were back on the wide plains of Honan Province, back in the garden behind the hospital, back at their own fireside. Little wonder Pearl was radiant, rejoicing, over-flowing with love—quite unconscious that she was astonishing everybody by her development in one short term!

It was a cold winter with plenty of snow, and the children found a delightful companion in the young missionary who had come to help in the business management of the hospital. When he could spare time, they all went skating or sledging, or running up and down the broad ascent to the city wall! When the lamps were lit in the evening and Mother had time to play games or read aloud, how they all enjoyed it in the cosy corner by the fire! Pearl herself was a great reader, but the Bible was the book she loved above all others; and the evening hour when Mother came up to read and pray with them before they went to sleep was looked forward to by all three with special delight. Mother had always done this, and no one could tell Bible stories or make it all so real and beautiful as she could. Then there was the Bible Searching Almanac, which was a great help in coming to know the Word of God for themselves. A text was given for every day, the chapter and verse of which had to be found. Only the name of the book was supplied, and it often meant patient search to discover the passage, but the children loved doing it, and Pearl did not tire as the months went on. Often she was to be seen poring over her Bible, reading chapter after chapter to find the special text, and then she would go to bed so happily when her search was rewarded.

But one night, strange to say, Pearl was not happy. Mother had left her with a good-night kiss as usual, wondering at the question her little girl had asked:

"Mother, how can we *know* that our names are written in the Lamb's book of life?"

The sweet voice had sounded troubled, and half an hour later her brother came down to say that Pearl was crying. Pearl, always so bright and happy—what could be the matter?

"It's about the name, Mother," she sobbed. "It's about the name. I can't go to sleep unless I *know.*"

She had been reading in Revelation, and the beauty of the heavenly city filled her heart. But it said so distinctly, "There shall in no wise enter into it any thing that defileth, neither whatsoever worketh abomination, or maketh a lie: *but they which are written in the Lamb's book of life*" (Rev. 21:27). Mother's name was written there, and Father's, and those of many whom she loved. But Pearl's name...? She had never really thought about it before. How could she know, oh, how could she be sure that her name was written there?

Wrapping her up warmly, Mother carried the troubled child to her own room and sat down to talk over the matter. The Spirit of God was moving, she could see, in this little heart, and He would give the light that alone could make the truth plain.

It was not about anything Pearl could do that Mother talked to her, but about what the Lord Jesus had done. When He bore all our sins on the dreadful cross, and cried aloud in the darkness, "It is finished," did that not mean that everything was finished that was needed for our salvation? Is He not "the Lamb of God that taketh away the sin of the world?" When we give our hearts to Him, He washes them whiter than snow; and He writes the names of all His own, all who trust Him, in the book of life.

"To have your name written there, darling, you need only to trust Jesus. As soon as you first began to love Him, He put your name in His book, and all you have to do—all anyone can do—is just to praise Him for it. Do you not want to kneel down now with Mother, and thank Him for having done this for you?"

O yes! That was just what Pearl wanted. She did love and trust Jesus, and she was so glad to understand that He really had written her name in His book of life.

"And now," Mother said when they had prayed together, "I want to give you a text to rest your heart on." Mother knew that even for little children it is what God says that brings strength and help. "Here it is—part of the first verse of Isaiah 43," and Mother read:

"Fear not: for I have redeemed thee, I have called thee by thy name; thou art mine."

Eagerly Pearl listened and repeated the words again and again. How sweet, how wonderful they were! Jesus knew her name, was calling her by her name. He had redeemed her. Her name must be in the book of life, for He said, "Thou art mine."

Very happily then, and peacefully, she went to sleep in the little camp bed Mother had made up beside her own. The precious words had so taken hold of her heart that she repeated them again and again after she was tucked up and Mother had said good-night. Then in the morning it all came back with a new flood of joy. She wanted to read the words again and borrowed Mother's Bible with references that she might find other passages that said the same thing—"Thou art mine." She was quite busy over it, turning to place after place and writing out the verses. And her little face was bright with a wonderfully sweet and tender light.

Nor was this all. A day or two later she was busy again for quite a long time. She had brought one of her treasures—a small, red leather pocket-book—and was bending over it, writing something that seemed to be of great importance. She did not show it to Mother, though she smiled at her across the table. Apparently it was a secret. But secrets were in the air just then, so near Christmas-time, and Mother asked no questions.

Was there ever a Christmas like that one, its hours freighted with happiness from morning to night? Carol singing, "stockings," visits to the bright wards of the hospital, a service in the decorated church, and so the day went on, full of the happiness of giving and receiving.

The New Year found Pearl poorly, though she was busy as usual—knitting little cuffs for the children of the Sunday School, and enjoying quiet reading and games. Father was watching his little daughter anxiously, and when the pain became worse and her temperature went up, he decided with the other doctors that there must be an operation. Pearl was not in the least afraid. As a little thing she had always been brave, and held up her head steadily whatever came, and now she seemed to be thinking more of others than herself.

"I shall soon come back," she said, looking so sweet and bright as they wrapped her up to carry her over to the hospital. And as she crossed the garden in the frosty air and sunshine, she called back:

"I like it, Mother, I like it!"

When the chloroform had to be given, she knew no fear. "It's all right, Father," she said trustfully, as he explained what he was doing. And she breathed it in with perfect quietness and went to sleep. Skilfully the operation was performed and the little patient tended, and Father hoped against hope that his precious child would recover. Things were very serious—but surely, surely that life so full of promise could not be near its close. But the Lord loved little Pearl better even than Father or Mother could, and He saw that it was best to take her to the Home above.

It had come so suddenly that the mother was almost stricken down with grief. Pearl lay still and silent—the dancing feet and willing hands no longer busy, the shining eyes closed, the loving lips without a word.

And then she remembered—Pearl's secret. Rising from the bedside, she went to find the pocket-book. There it was, safely put away among other treasures. Opening it, Mother found in childish writing just the message her heart needed. Her child was speaking to her from the borders of the Better Land. She read and read again, with tears of thankfulness:

"Pearl gave her heart to the Lord on December 14, 1918, aged eight years. Her text was: 'Fear not: for I have redeemed thee, I have called thee by thy name; thou art mine.'"

The night was dark—but not for little Pearl. For her the morning light was dawning, and all the wonderful, sweet meaning of her secret.

What about me?

"Fear not, for I have redeemed you; I have summoned you by name; you are mine. When you pass through the waters, I will be with you; and when you pass through the rivers, they will not sweep over you. When you walk through the fire, you will not be burned; the flames will not set you ablaze. For I am the Lord, your God, the Holy One of Israel, your Saviour" (Isaiah 43:1-3).

There are times in every person's life when they don't feel too sure about something. It is often easy to be unsure of God, because we cannot see Him, and we don't always feel like He is there. Are there ever times when I don't really know if God is with me? Do those times drive me away from God, or do they help me to come closer to Him? Does the Bible say anything to me when I am not sure whether God loves me, or if I really am His child? How can I know that I have come into a strong and sure friendship with almighty God? (For further study you can read John 3:16; Philippians 1:3-6.)

Heavenly Father,
Because of the wonderful gift of your Son, Jesus Christ, I can know that my sins are forgiven and that I have become your child. Help me to always remember that your love and forgiveness is much bigger than my sin, and that you have done everything to bring me into everlasting, heavenly life, if I will only believe in Jesus and His finished work on the cross. Amen.

The Obstinate Horse

GRANDFATHER Ma was a Moslem, a proud wealthy Chinese farmer. The countryside was most unpeaceful, with generals and soldiers always fighting each other, riding their horses over the growing crops, living in the farmers' homes, and helping themselves to what they liked. Some months previously the Ma farmstead had had a company of soldiers, really bandits, lodged in it, and was much the poorer for it. But it was no use complaining to the company officer, for he could not control his men, nor did he care in the least what they did or how much they stole.

Ma Ling May, eight years old, was the old gentleman's little granddaughter. Her parents had allowed her to go to a Christian school, and there she had come truly to love the Lord Jesus, yet nothing made her grandfather more angry than to hear the name of Jesus mentioned, or to know that Ling May prayed to God. "He would have no such doings in his house," he roared;

and if ever he found her praying he would beat and kick the child. But Ling May kept on, and felt sure that somehow God would find a way to change her grandfather's heart.

One day while Mr. Ma was taking a walk on the city wall, which was as wide as a road, he got a terrible fright —for there in the distance he saw the band of soldiers who had plundered the city some months ago, now heading for it again; yes, he recognised the same general riding at their head!

What was he to do? He felt sure the soldiers were coming back to ransack his house, knowing it to be the wealthiest and best stocked with food and clothes and everything. There wasn't a hope for him. *Wasn't there?* He suddenly thought of Ling May. Didn't she pray to God and say that He heard and answered? Hurrying home he found her, shook her roughly, and almost yelled, "If ever you prayed in your life, pray now! Those soldiers are coming back. I have seen them from the city wall; they will soon be here. You say your God answers prayer. Go into that room and pray that they may not come to our house!"

He pushed the child into an empty room and banged the door. All alone the little girl knelt down. Her mother who was in the next room, heard her as she called upon God to help. "Heavenly Father," she said, "I am so happy, so thankful because Grandfather has told me to pray. Before he has always beaten or kicked me if I prayed, and was so angry, but now he has told me to pray. Heavenly Father, *now's Your chance!* Please show my Grandfather that You do answer prayer. PLEASE don't let the soldiers come to our house; I ask this in Jesus' Name."

The soldiers entered the city and came tramping down that very street. The gate of grandfather's house was standing open—a huge wooden door leading into the courtyard—for he knew it would be of no use to shut it. The officer in front of the band drew up and turned his horse's head to go in. That was the place he was making for all right. And the little girl inside was praying, "Don't let them come into our house. Heavenly Father, now's Your chance! Please show my grandfather that You do answer prayer."

Was she answered? Yes! Something happened; perhaps the last thing one would have thought of. Most surprisingly the horse would not go in; no, it backed and kicked; it shied this way and that, and nothing would make it go in. The officer beat it, and dug his spurs into it, but it was no use. *It would not go in.* Then the officer turned to his men and said, "Why, this court-yard must be full of demons; we cannot see them, but the horse can. Not one of you is to go in there, not one!" And he turned his horse and led his men to another part of the town.

What the horse saw or shied at we do not know, but we do know that long ago there was a donkey who absolutely refused to go forward, even though its master Balaam beat it hard three times, because although the man saw nothing, the donkey saw the Angel of the Lord standing with a drawn sword blocking the path. You can read about that in the Old Testament Book of Numbers, chapter twenty-two.

The next day the grandfather went round to the Mission house, and when he saw the missionary he said with true humility, "To think that all the while that little granddaughter of mine was right, and I was wrong. Teach me about the God who answers prayer like that. Teach me to pray."

What about me?

"The Lord is a refuge for the oppressed, a stronghold in times of trouble. Those who know your name will trust in you, for you, Jehovah, have never forsaken those who seek you" (Psalm 9:9-10).

Many people in the world have forgotten that God exists. They do not pray, and they do not want Him to have any part in their lives. How do I feel when I am in the middle of those people? Do I still trust God when nobody else around me does? Do I really know that God will answer my prayers? What would I do if praying was going to cost me something? (For further study you can read Daniel 6:1-24.)

Heavenly Father,
Sometimes I feel alone when I pray. I often feel like nobody else understands or even thinks that you will hear me. Some people even try to stop me from praying. In those times, help me to keep my eyes on you and to remember that you often choose things that seem impossible to show just how mighty you are. Help me to never give up praying and never lose hope for those people around me who haven't seen how wonderful you are yet. Please show yourself to me and to them, for your glory. Amen.

10

A Table in the Wilderness

TWO missionaries were camped on a high plateau between ranges of snow-clad mountains somewhere in Central Asia. Hanging up in their tent was a "Cheering Words" calendar, and the text for the day had impressed Percy Mather, the younger of the two missionaries, for he had just been checking up their food stores. They had 5 lb. of flour, 5 lb. rice, 1 lb. lentils, and 2 lb. butter. No meat, no milk, no eggs, no vegetables, and no prospect of obtaining any, for they had not passed a town or even a hamlet for days, and now they were unable to travel onwards because their Mongol servant was at death's door with typhoid fever! No wonder that the text on the calendar for that day seemed chosen to cheer and encourage them. It read: "Consider the ravens; for they neither sow nor reap, which neither have storehouse nor barn; and God feedeth them; how much more are ye better than the fowls?" (Luke 12:24). Underneath the text was printed a little verse:

> "The raven He feedeth, then why should I fear?
> To the heart of the Father His children are dear;
> So if the way darkens, or storms gather o'er,
> I'll simply look upward, and trust Him the more."

Percy Mather felt that, in their circumstances, those were cheering words indeed. With their food running out, their fuel of grass and horse dung wet with rain, and the prospect of being held up in this desert place for some weeks to come looking after their ill servant, it was good indeed to be reassured of God's care for His children. Now in their extremity what would He do? The following quotations from Percy Mather's diary provide the answer.

July 17. Bright, frosty morning. Ground covered with hailstones. Four ravens flying round our camp.

July 18. The text in "Cheering Words" calendar, Psalm 9:9,10. "The Lord also will be a refuge for the oppressed, a refuge in times of trouble. And they that know Thy name will put their trust in Thee: for Thou, Lord, hast not forsaken them that seek Thee." Fine frosty morning again, all hands busy gathering fuel. At breakfast I said to our other servant boy, "We have only two more basins of rice and one of lentils." He looked very downhearted until I added, "AND GOD"; then he cheered up a bit. Today while gathering grass and fuel that text of Scripture came forcefully into my mind:

"Can God prepare a table in the wilderness?"

I had to stop and laugh when I thought of it—yet not a laugh of doubt, but of faith. The text seems a direct challenge to God. Here we are held up in this wilderness with only two basins of rice and one of lentils. *Can* God prepare a table in the wilderness?

10 am: While gathering fuel was surprised and delighted to see an English army officer with two Indian servants coming towards our tent. It was Colonel Schonberg, of the Indian Army, who had seen our tent from a distance, and leaving the main road had come to inspect. We had met before, so needed no introduction. The previous night he had camped not far from our tent, but neither of us knew it. He said, "I intended going on, but will now stop and enjoy some English society—that is, if you will have me." Shortly afterwards his caravan arrived with

his other servants. Three or four tents were pitched near ours, and we seemed quite a little village. The Colonel said, "Please come along in half an hour and have a cup of tea with me." We went and found tea, bread and butter, cheese, jam, and *a table!* You can imagine how vividly my text came into my mind once again. During our conversation the Colonel said, "Now to be practical, what can I give you in the way of stores?" We made a modest request, but we soon found he was able to give us far more than we dared ask or imagine: tinned milk, Allenbury's malted food, and medicines for our ill Mongol servant; rice, flour, sugar, butter, cheese, cocoa, damson jam, baking powder, arrowroot, and, what pleased me tremendously, a tin of Lyle's golden syrup!

In the evening the Colonel invited us to dinner. A wild wind was blowing, and the cook had great difficulty with the fire, but he made us a splendid dinner, which we thoroughly enjoyed, not having had any meat or vegetables for over a fortnight.

MENU

Soup. . . . Kidney
Hot dish. . . . Mutton chops
Vegetables. . . . Potatoes, carrots, kidney beans
Dessert. . . . Blancmange and apricots
Dutch cheese
Coffee and tea

July 19. "Cheering Words" text. Isaiah 35:6. "In the wilderness shall waters break out and streams in the desert." Colonel Schonberg invited us to a farewell breakfast. Afterwards he took the height of our camp with a hypsometer and found it to be 9,500 feet.

10 am: Said "Goodbye" to our kind friend and watched him out of sight. By this time the Mongols down the valley had heard of us and came for medicine, bringing with them presents of milk, butter, and cheese, etc. Then some Turki merchants sold us some of their rice, on condition that we directed them a few miles along the road. Another traveller with a flock of sheep sold us one that had become lame, and killed and prepared it for us. So now we had plenty for ourselves, and some to spare for occasional Mongol and desert guests who might spend the night with us.

"Can God prepare a table in the wilderness?"
YES! HE CAN!

What about me?

"Therefore, I tell you, do not worry about your life, what you will eat or drink; or about your body, what you will wear. Is not life more important than food, and the body more important than clothes? Look at the birds of the air; they do not sow or reap or store away in barns, and yet your heavenly Father feeds them. Are you not much more valuable than they?" (Matthew 6:25-26).

All around me people say that humans are really just intelligent animals, that we are only very clever machines that happen to have feelings—at least sometimes. It is easy to feel like I have no real reason to be here or that I am not very important. But God knows everything about me, and He cares enough to give me everything that I need, even in out of the way places. Do I ever stop to think about how important I am to God? Do I know that even my smallest problems are always before His all-seeing eyes? Do I really take time to thank Him for the good things He gives me every day, even when I do not see when He is at work in my life? (For further study you can read Matthew 6:28-34.)

Heavenly Father,
So many people spend their whole lives trying to get as many things as they can. They are always worried about what they do or don't have. Help me to understand that you know everything that I need, and that you are always watching over me—in good times and bad. Help me to trust you enough to put my needs, and my wants, into your hands. If I put you first, I know that you will take care of me. Amen.

Fed by Ravens

MR. Lee had stopped worshipping idols, and was now whole-heartedly trusting God. He heard a sermon once based on the text, "Covetousness which is idolatry." This gave him quite a fright, so much so that he decided to give away his money and property in case these should occupy too big a place in his heart. "For then," he thought, "if I coveted or loved possessions I should be like an idolater again." So he handed over his little house and farm to a nephew, and spent his whole time telling the people of his neighbourhood about the Gospel, becoming the pastor of a small church. Then after a while he opened a home where people who wanted to break off smoking opium could come and be looked after by him. Gradually his money was used up and he ran short of what he needed, and his faith in God was truly tested.

Nearby in the large temple of the village lived a cousin of Lee's who was priest-in-charge, and who, when he came to visit his relative from time to time, would bring a little present of bread or millet from his ample store. The old man, on receiving these gifts, would always say, "It is my Heavenly Father's grace," meaning that it was through the care and kindness of God that these gifts were brought. But the priest did not agree to that way of looking at it, and at last said, "Where does your Heavenly Father's grace come in, I should like to know? The millet is mine. I bring it to you, and if I did not, you would soon starve for all that He would care. He has nothing at all to do with it."

"But it is my Heavenly Father who puts it into your heart to care for me," replied Lee.

"Oh, that's all very well," interrupted the priest. "We shall see what will happen if I bring no more millet." For a week or two he kept away, although his conscience told him he ought to care for the old man whom he really admired for all the kind and helpful things he did for other people.

This was just at a time when old Lee was especially short of supplies. At last there came a day when he had nothing left for another meal, and no money to buy any bread. Kneeling alone in his room, he brought all his troubles to God, feeling certain that his Father in heaven would not, could not forget him. He prayed for the people all round him and asked that God for His own great Name's sake would send him that day his daily bread, and so prove to the temple priest that God truly cared and would provide for him.

Then and there the answer came. While the old man was still kneeling in prayer he heard an unusual clamour and cawing and flapping of wings in the courtyard outside, and a noise as of something falling to the ground. He rose and went to the door to see what was happening. A number of ravens, which are common in that part of China, were flying about in great commotion above him, and as he looked up a large piece of fat pork fell at his very feet. One of the birds, chased by the others, had dropped it just at that moment on that spot.

Thankfully the old man took up the unexpected meat, saying, "It is my Heavenly Father's kindness." And then, glancing about him to see what he had heard fall before he came out, he discovered a large piece of bread, all cooked and ready for eating. Another bird had dropped that also—and there was his dinner bountifully provided! Evidently the ravens had been on a stealing expedition and, overtaken by stronger birds, had let go their booty. But whose hand had guided them to drop their prize right above his little courtyard?

With a heart overflowing with joy and amazement, Mr. Lee lit a fire to prepare the welcome meal; and while the pot was still boiling the door opened, and, to his great delight, his cousin the priest walked in.

"Well, has your Heavenly Father sent you anything to eat?" he asked with a scornful smile, keeping a bag of millet he had brought carefully hidden up his sleeve.

"Look and see," replied the old man, smiling, as he pointed to the saucepan simmering on the fire.

For some time the priest would not lift the lid, feeling sure there was nothing boiling there but water, but when a delicious smell was unmistakable, overcome by curiosity he peeped into the pot. What was his astonishment to see the large piece of juicy fat pork! "Why," he cried, "where did you get this?" "My Heavenly Father sent it," responded the old man delightedly. "He put it into your heart, you know, to bring me a little millet from time to time, but when you would no longer do so, it was quite easy for Him to find another messenger." Mr. Lee told his cousin all the story, about his prayer and about the coming of the ravens.

The priest was so much impressed by what he saw and heard that he began to inquire more fully about his cousin's God, and later he himself believed in the Lord Jesus and was baptised. He gave up his comfortable living in the temple, and earned his living as a teacher, and became a deacon in the church. During the fierce anti-Christian riots some years later, he bravely endured terrible tortures, and finally laid down his life for Jesus' sake.

What about me?

"Ah, Sovereign Lord, you have made the heavens and the earth by your great power and outstretched arm. Nothing is too hard for you" (Jeremiah 32:17).

Many people today don't have room in their lives for God. They say He isn't real, and that anybody that believes in Him is only chasing an empty dream. Yet God still does amazing things in the lives of normal people who choose to put their faith and trust in Him, people just like me. When I think about God, what do I think He is like? Do I think He is all-powerful, or do I think of Him more as a nice old man? How often have I asked God to show His power in my life? Am I willing to take a chance and trust Him with every part of my life? Do I think He is able to do it? (For further study you can read 2 Kings 4:1-7.)

Heavenly Father,

You made the earth and everything that is in it. How mighty and wonderful you must be! No problem is too big for you, nor is any problem too small. Even the small things in the life of normal people seem to get your attention. Help me to remember just how great and powerful you are. Teach me to learn the lesson that you are interested in every part of my life and that I should bring every part of my world to you in prayer. Then you can show yourself to me and all those around me. Amen.

The Lost Hen

MRS. Tang had a hen which laid an egg every other day. She prayed that the hen should lay an egg *every* day, and decided when her prayer was answered to give every tenth egg to the Lord.

One day she came to the missionary in great distress, saying, "Missionary, do pray with me that the Lord will help me, that my hen will return, for it is lost." We prayed; but the next day the woman came again and said, "The hen has not returned, do let's pray again." We did so, but still it did not return. The third morning she said sorrowfully, "No sign of it yet." Should we keep on praying? The hen may have been killed and eaten—if so it would be foolish to go on asking God that it might be found. The woman came again the fourth morning; I wanted to give her money to buy another hen, and yet felt it would be better to wait and see how this matter turned out. On the fifth morning, and on the sixth, there was still nothing to report. Mrs. Tang said, "I do not know why the Lord does not answer our prayers, but I feel sure it will be returned to me." We prayed again, and Mrs. Tang turned homewards, saying to herself, "Lord, where is my hen?" As she passed slowly along the street, she suddenly spied a woman with a hen hidden under her arm, on her way to market, and at once Mrs. Tang called out, "That's my hen! You shall not sell it!" But the other woman insisted it was hers, and so an argument began, and a crowd gathered round to listen.

Then someone said to the Christian woman, "Go to the Headman of the street; he will decide to whom the hen belongs." They went to the man concerned, but how was he to decide? The Christian woman prayed, "Lord, help the Headman to understand that it is my hen." The Headman asked the other woman how long she had had the hen. She answered, "I bought it when it was a chick, and have watched it grow. Now it is fat, I want to sell it, as I need money." Then he turned to the Christian and asked how long she had had it. "I bought it when it was very tiny, and looked after it, and for a long time it has laid an egg every day, but I lost it six days ago. I am quite sure it is mine." All were wondering how the referee would decide. The Christian woman kept on praying in her heart, "Lord, show him it is mine."

The crowd waited interestedly. The Headman said to the other woman, "Put the hen here. Go over to the corner and call it." The woman did so and called, "Tututu," but the hen did not move. She called again, but in vain. Now the referee said to the Christian woman, "You go and call it." While walking across to the place, she kept saying to herself, "Lord, when I call, let it come to me, because it is mine." When she called, "Tututu," the hen lifted its head and slowly went across to her. The official said to the other woman, "Go! or I will put you in prison. The hen knows to whom it belongs."

Mrs. Tang was so happy, and came to tell us at once. Three

days later she told this affair in the church, and put three eggs and some money on the table at the front, saying, "This I give as a thank-offering to the Lord for answering my prayers."

What about me?

"Ask and it will be given to you; seek and you will find; knock and the door will be opened to you. For everyone who asks receives; he who seeks finds; and to him who knocks, the door will be opened.

"Which of you, if his son asks for bread, will give him a stone? Or if he asks for a fish, will give him a snake? If you, then, though you are evil, know how to give good gifts to your children, how much more will your Father in heaven give good gifts to those who ask him!" (Matthew 7:7-11).

I'm not always very good at waiting for things. I like to have what I want right now. But God doesn't always work in the way or at the time that I want. Am I learning that God sometimes waits so that I can learn to be patient and not give up? Do I understand that He knows not only *what* is best for me but also *when* is best for me? Have I learned enough about Him to know that He always does what is best for me, even if I don't understand what He is doing, or why He seems to be taking so long? Do I keep trusting and keep asking? How does God see it when I keep praying about something? (For further study you can read Luke 18:1-8.)

Heavenly Father,

Not giving up is a hard lesson to learn, especially when it comes to praying about things. Sometimes asking you more than once helps me to learn just how much I really do need you. Please help me to be patient and faithful and not to give up, because I know that you are a God who rewards those who keep looking for you. Amen.

13

A Chicken Flew Over the Wall

JAPANESE troops were near. The city of Road of Peace was desolate, especially since the mayor and city officials had moved out to the mountain village off the main route and insisted that the whole population move too, taking all their goods and chattels with them. So the butcher, the baker, the candlestick maker with wives and families, furniture, stock-in-trade, even the wooden doors and wooden counters of their shops, had all been carted up to the mountains where the enemy was most unlikely to try to follow them. And of course such prized members of the family as the pig and the chickens were driven or carried squawking along too.

So now all was silent, ominously silent, in the empty shell of the city, waiting for the rattle of machine guns. No, not quite empty, for the mission compound had not evacuated; a few missionary families, the hospital staff, and some servants who were brave enough to stay on, were there. During the weeks of rumours of the advancing enemy they were busy trying to get in stores of grain and flour in preparation for the time of siege. Then the Japanese planes zoomed low over the empty city and, unchallenged, dropped bombs at will. In the hour's interval between two raids one morning, a tiny missionary baby was born and promptly did her first hiding from enemy action on a straw mattress under her mother's bed.

The capable nurse was hard put to it to find the right kind of food for her patient. No butchers' shops were open now; no meat of any kind was procurable. Just when the baby's mother was most in need of tasty, strengthening food, it seemed there was none to give her. The city was empty, the store cupboard too, like that of Mother Hubbard's, was almost bare. Then, when the baby was just two days old, the nurse walked into the bedroom with a bowl of steaming chicken broth. *Chicken* broth! Following her, full of excitement, were the cook and the woman servant, eager to see what the patient would say when she tasted this unexpected meal. *Chicken* broth! Where had they got the chicken?

They told her. . . . A chicken had flown over the wall that very morning! Does it sound an ordinary happening? It was most extraordinary! What Chinese would leave a precious chicken behind when fleeing to the mountains from the Japanese invaders? How could a chicken have flown over that twenty-foot wall? And where could it have come from? On the other side of that wall was merely field after field of corn stalks. All the Chinese servants were closely questioned, but none of them claimed it. There was only one explanation of the mystery. The God who commanded the ravens to feed Elijah could command chickens too!

What about me?

"But he said to me, 'My grace is sufficient for you, for my power is made perfect in weakness.' Therefore I will boast all the more gladly about my weaknesses, so that Christ's power may rest on me. That is why, for Christ's sake, I delight in weaknesses, in insults, in persecutions, in difficulties. For when I am weak, then I am strong" (2 Corinthians 12:9-10).

In my world it is important for people to be strong. The strong person is always thought of as the one who is the winner, the best. Yet sometimes being weak opens the way for God to do something really incredible! How do I feel when I am in the middle of a problem that is much bigger than I am? Do I panic? Do I start fighting to find a way out? Do I ever stop and turn to God and ask Him to help me when I don't feel very strong? Do I ever thank Him for the hard times, like Paul did, because then I know He is going to show me something incredible about himself? (For further study you can read 1 Kings 17:1-6.)

Heavenly Father,

Nobody is stronger than you. Yet many times I feel like I need to show everybody how strong I am. The truth is I want to do things on my own, but many times I can't. When I feel weak and helpless, help me to turn to you and remember that you are able to help me in my weakness. No matter how difficult the problem, you always have an answer, even when I can't see an answer. Help me remember that when I am weak, you are always strong. Amen.

14

The Farmer's Field

TO millions of people in China rice is the staff of life, so much so that they speak of it as "the little white gems." Rice grows in water. In the spring farmers are busy from morning till night preparing the ground. Just when the fields need to be flooded heavy rains may be expected. Then the young rice plant is sown by hand, about ten inches apart, and every root clump is carefully attended to until the rice harvest about two months later.

If a Chinese is asked, "Where do you get your rice from?", he usually answers by a well-known proverb which says, "Heaven gave me life, and Heaven sends me rice." Occasionally the rain fails to come, then the days are blisteringly hot, and the fields cracked with drought. Most villages have a large pond or reservoir where water is stored for such an emergency. By using an endless chain of wooden scoops, water is raised to the level of the prepared fields which have ditches dug between them. This endless chain can only be revolved and kept revolving by means of men treading it, and this hard job is called "treading the waters." As the water flows along the channels between the fields, a little break is made in the raised edge of the field and the water flows in to flood the whole field; then the opened part is banked up again, and the next field gets its share. Each farmer sharing in the reservoir is allotted a certain day or days to water his fields.

In a certain village there lived a Christian farmer who was often mocked by his heathen neighbours. One year the rice fields were becoming parched, and the villagers decided to begin to use the precious stored water, so each family was allowed to take their share in treading the water for a certain length of time. The following day was Sunday, and the villagers planned that the Christian farmer should take his share of water during the time that he would ordinarily be away in the city worshipping God, along with other Christians.

"Let us see what his religion amounts to," someone said. "Will he risk losing his share of the water for the sake of worshipping the foreign God?" said others.

As the Sunday morning dawned, to the surprise of the villagers, they saw this quiet Christian farmer leave his home carrying his little bag with Bible and hymn book and his midday meal, just as usual, and leave for the city.

After the service the farmer told the congregation about the unfair watering situation and asked his friends to pray that God would help him in some special way. By the time they should go home, great clouds began to gather, and all the people said excitedly, "The rain is coming! The rain is coming!" Sure enough, before the farmer could reach his home a tremendous downpour flooded the countryside. He noticed that some of the fields of those who had stolen his water were too full now with the rain, and water poured off them carrying much rice with it, ruining the crop. His own fields were just well filled, with none running over. How he praised his Heavenly Father, not only for such a wonderful water supply, but also for watering his fields for him, and saving him all the hard treading work! And he proved, too, that God's promise is true: "Them that honour Me, I will honour" (1 Samuel 2:30). The neighbours were all most impressed, and no wonder!

What about me?

"Whoever serves me must follow me; and where I am, my servant also will be. My Father will honour the one who serves me" (John 12:26).

Obeying God can be risky—especially when everyone around me wants to see me fail. How important to me is following God? Is doing what He wants me to do the most important thing in my life? Do I trust Him to take care of me when my obeying Him looks crazy to all those around me? Do I truly believe that He will reward me if I am faithful to Him? (For further study you can read Daniel 1:3-20.)

Heavenly Father,
Doing what pleases you can be hard. Sometimes I feel like I'm all alone and going to fail. In those times, please help me to remember that you are always watching me, and that you reward those who do things your way. If it means taking a risk, help me remember that you always make every risk totally worthwhile! Amen.

(15)

The Lost Well

MRS. Wu was on a visit to her married sister Mrs. Sun, and enjoying it very much. Not only was it good to be together again, but she was very interested to hear her sister talk of a true God and His Son Jesus Christ, whom she was now worshipping. Also, she heard her sister speak to this God as though He was quite near and could hear her.

After she returned home, as Mrs. Wu lay in bed one night, she thought it all over. She would find out for sure if this God her sister believed in was really true. She knew of a way she could prove it. . . if this God could solve the mystery of the lost well, she too would believe in Him.

A good water supply is very valuable in China. In the Wu home it had to be bought by the barrelful from water carriers, and it was not good water at that; it had a bitter taste. Mrs. Wu had often longed for a pure water supply, and she knew that in the old family register was a record of a well that was in the back yard of the property on which their house was built. Years ago she had told her two sisters about this lost well, and in odd moments they dug and hunted for traces of it, but in vain. The ground had been a vegetable garden for as long as the present generation could remember, and so the quest was abandoned.

As Mrs. Wu lay wondering, she really did want to know what was true. Was there a loving Heavenly Father as her sister said?

Did He want her for His child? She had never prayed except to idols, to which one must first burn incense, kill a chicken, and sprinkle its blood before the idol. But her sister had said that if we trust in Jesus Christ we can pray to God without fear. Now Mrs. Wu prayed for the first time, "O God, if you are the true God, reveal to me this night the place of the well, and I will be your child." Later that night she had a dream and seemed to hear a voice say to her, "The well is directly opposite the big back door, in such and such a spot."

The next morning Mrs. Wu rose early and, calling a little servant girl, went into the garden. "Come," she said, "the well is here, and we will dig." First they removed a pile of rubbish, then dug down a foot of earth. A big brick was revealed, then more bricks in the shape of a circle—they were the stones covering the opening of a well! A great thrill of joy filled Mrs. Wu, and she exclaimed aloud, "O God, I am your child!"

When the well was cleaned out it was found to be fourteen feet deep, lined all the way with brick, and what was more, there was a good supply of clear, fresh water. Best of all, Mrs. Wu very soon found the source of the Water of Life, Jesus Christ, the Son of God.

What about me?

"'For I know the plans I have for you,' declares the Lord, 'plans to prosper you and not to harm you, plans to give you hope and a future. Then you will call upon me and come and pray to me, and I will listen to you. You will seek me and find me when you seek me with all your heart" (Jeremiah 29:11-13).

God never forces himself on anyone. But He is always there—watching and waiting for us to call on Him, to seek Him, to make the first steps to really know Him. Do I believe God can give me the kind of life that He promises? How often do I come to Him and really call to Him in prayer? Can I truly say that I have made the steps to find Him and to know His love in my heart? (For further study you can read John 10:1-10.)

Heavenly Father,
I understand that everyone has to get to know you for them-selves. I can't rely on my dad or my mom, or my brother or sister to look for you. I have to look for you with all my heart if I truly want to know you. Please touch my heart and help me to know you and the wonderful life that you have for me in Jesus Christ. Amen.

(16)

Buffy Rat Rips a Poster

BUFFY Rat just managed to drag his long tail in behind him under the brick leading to the drain before Belle Miao Cat saw him. She was too late that time! "Guess I'll go up the drain into Granny Tong's yard," he said. "But she always sweeps the chapel out clean just as soon as the people go away from church. I do wish she would leave the peanut shells there, for the children drop lots of titbits I could eat."

So Buffy Rat went on up the drain and came into Granny Tong's well-swept yard. He turned and looked around to see if Belle Miao Cat was anywhere around; at the same time he looked at the wall to find a good place to scramble over in case she did come along later. Then he ran as fast as he could to the chapel. Sure enough, it was all swept and clean. There was not a peanut to be seen anywhere, nor a scrap of bread. Nothing had been left on the table against the wall, not a crumb could be found on the chair. He ran up the chair leg, jumped on to the table, and sniffed behind some hymn books, but not a thing could he find.

Just then he looked up at the big gospel picture poster on the wall and sniffed again. "Why, of course," he said, "there is flour paste on the back of that picture, and that would be quite a mouthful." He stretched up on his two hind legs, and then started to climb gingerly up to the top of the picture. Just as he began to nibble at the top corner, he heard a frightful noise. He thought it must be Belle Miao Cat coming after him, so, taking a bite in the corner of the poster, he jumped down, tearing a long strip of the paper after him. "I can't stop to eat it now," he thought, "but I'll take it home, eat the paste, and use the paper for my bedding." So Buffy scrambled off the table and, dragging the long piece of paper behind him, scampered along for all he was worth to try to get over the wall to the street and home before Belle Miao Cat could find him.

Now it happened that an old man with a cane was walking down the street just then. Coming over the wall, Buffy saw the man lift his cane to hit him. That scared him so much that he dropped the paper and ran for his life, leaving the long strip of paper at the feet of the old man. Buffy did not know that the strip of paper had some Chinese words on it which said, "Christ Jesus came into the world to save sinners, of whom I am chief." Neither did he wait to see the old man pick up the paper and read it. "This is strange," the man thought. "I am the worst of sinners, but who is Christ Jesus?"

He walked along and turned a corner, and there on the door of a hall he read the very same words! "Perhaps He lives here," he said to himself. "I'll go in and find out who this person is." So he walked into the courtyard where Buffy had been, just in time to find Granny Tong coming out of her house.

"Does Christ Jesus live in this place?" he asked. "Please come in, and we will tell you about Him," she answered. Then she led the old man into her guest room and poured her visitor a cup of tea. Granny Tong and her husband explained to the old man who Christ Jesus is, and how He had come to this earth to save sinners. Before they had finished talking, the old man was ready to believe that the Lord would save him from his sins too, and felt so happy when Mr. Tong prayed for him.

So the strip of paper torn from the chapel wall did more good than if Buffy Rat had used it to line his bed after all.

基督耶穌降世為要拯救罪人

What about me?

"The Lord is not slow in keeping his promise, as some understand slowness. He is patient with you, not wanting anyone to perish, but everyone to come to repentance" (2 Peter 3:9).

I know many people who have never met Jesus. Without Him they don't know what it means to have life that lasts forever. God really wants them to know about Him and what Jesus did for them. He will do some amazing things to make sure they find out. How much do I care that my friends don't know Jesus? How often do I pray for them? Do I ever tell them about Jesus and what He did for them? Do I ever ask God to help them to find Him? Do I really think that He will answer? What would I do to bring a friend of mine to Jesus? (For further study you can read Luke 5:17-26.)

Heavenly Father,

I am glad that you want everyone to know you and all that you have done for them through your son, Jesus. I know that you love my friends and family much more than I can understand. Help me also to love them and to help those who don't know you to see how much you care for them. Give me courage to do or say whatever will help them to learn more about you and how wonderful you really are. Amen.

God's Easy Way

SEVERAL hundred years ago someone afraid of the Yellow River flood waters built a tall narrow building. It was a rather ugly brick place jutting high above the mud houses all around. Then it was rumoured that ghosts had gone to live in the place, and it was left empty for a long time. Eventually some missionaries came to the town, and as they were not in the slightest afraid of ghosts or evil spirits, they bought the tall building for their home.

War, followed by a terrible famine, came to the province of China which lies just south of the great Yellow River. One of the missionaries living there at the time tells how "Four of us were in our tall home and knew well enough of the famine conditions around us. Day after day all we could get was carrots, cabbage, and spinach. Sugar, meat, eggs, flour, and even salt, were luxuries, and we were often hungry.

"On the roof of our tower roosted a large number of pigeons. Many a time we thought what a good meal we could make of them! We prayed about it, and I set out to find a way to catch some of them. I tried a slingshot, but could scarcely hit the house, let alone the pigeons! Someone else had an idea to lean out of the top storey and fling out a rope weighted with a heavy piece of wood, hoping to hit some of the birds—but it was no use at all. Later, a Chinese girl made a snare net of hair,

in which she hid grains of wheat, but the pigeons would not venture near it.

"One day as I came down the path and realised how all our methods had failed, I looked up at those pigeons again and asked our Heavenly Father to let us have some, for it was a long time since we had tasted meat. A snowstorm came, and I forgot the pigeons. The snow was followed by a fierce wind, and during the night everything froze. Early next morning I heard someone calling from downstairs, 'Do you want any pigeons?' I looked out, and there scattered about were the frozen birds, fallen to the ground. In less time than it takes to tell this, we hurried out and picked up nine pigeons straightaway. What a delicious dinner we had that day!"

What about me?

"And my God will supply all your needs according to his glorious riches in Christ Jesus" (Philippians 4:19).

Sometimes I feel like the things that I want to ask God are silly and unimportant. But God already knows everything that I am thinking and all that is going on in my life. Do I realise that He wants to be my heavenly Father? Do I understand that He is able to take care of every problem, even the things that might not seem very important? Have I learned the lesson that He is a good God who has control of everything in the universe? Am I learning just how much He loves every one of His children, even me? (For further study you can read Exodus 16.)

Heavenly Father,

It is amazing to me that the world and everything in it belongs to you. Sometimes you seem so big, and I seem so very small. Still, you have shown your people over and over that if they come to you with a heart that wants to believe, you will do truly remarkable things for them. Help me to always remember how great you truly are, and just how much you love me and how much you want to give me every good gift as I learn to walk with you. Amen.

(18)

The Strangest Flock I Ever Saw

"Make no mistake about it: *'Bad company is the ruin of Good Character.'*" Of course I had always been told this from the time I was a child, but somehow one does not believe all that one is told, and most youngsters leave home feeling that for them, at any rate, such a warning is unnecessary and can be discarded along with the other copies written in the nursery books. As a matter of fact I was quite grown up before I saw something which made me understand the truth of this proverb, but when I did see it, there was a picture imprinted on my mind very like the impression made on a negative when the camera exposes a film. It was there for good.

I was staying with friends in a ravine in the north of China, and one morning, wandering out before the others were up, I came across a shepherd who led the very strangest looking flock I have ever seen. Not one of his sheep was whole; broken legs, dislocated shoulders, and every kind of deformity was to be seen among them. I could not think that he had been cruel to them, for he seemed to be a specially nice fellow, so I asked him why he had such a strange flock all to himself.

"Well," he said, "these valleys are treacherous places. The hills have tempting bits of green hanging over, and when the goats climb into dangerous places the sheep follow them."

"But you have no goats in this flock," I said, "and anyway you surely do not pasture sheep and goats together."

"That is just what we did," he answered, "and that is why our sheep have come to grief. Goats, you see, are nimble creatures and can look after themselves. They make nothing of those rocks and crevices and can climb anywhere with safety. They just leap across the chasms and always manage to secure a foothold. They are so strong that no harm comes to them."

"What has that to do with these sheep?" I asked, looking round at the pitiful creatures.

"Well," he said, "the sheep will follow the goats, instead of staying down here with me in the green pastures. When they see a goat heading for some high place, before I can stop them, off they go, and the next thing is a tumble and a broken leg. All these sheep have come to grief that way."

I thought to myself: "That is what it meant, 'Bad company is the Ruin of Good Character.' The copy book was right after all."

There is something so different about sheep and goats that they ought not even to be feeding together, but when they are thrown into each other's company, let the sheep remember that *what is safe for goats is dangerous for sheep.*

The Lord Jesus called His people sheep, and the only safe place for you and me is near to the Good Shepherd. If we go wandering off with goats, we shall certainly get hurt, and though He will lovingly take us back to His flock and care for us, we may find ourselves with something broken that will never quite heal again, and we shall be maimed for life.

The place for the sheep is in the green pastures, near to the Shepherd, and when He sends one of them out, He Himself has said that He will go before them. If He is ahead, you will not get into any trouble, for He will be there to lead you.

What about me?

"Do not be misled: 'Bad company corrupts good character'" (1 Corinthians 15:33).

Sometimes it is hard not to be like everybody else. People tell me I should be doing this or doing that. But not everybody that wants me to follow them is going the right way. Do I ever stop and think about what my friends are doing, or who I am following? Would I ever do something that I know is wrong just to keep my friends or to look good to them? Do I make sure that I try to see everything in my life the way that God sees it, and do I keep away from the things and the people that could lead me in the wrong way? (For further study you can read Psalm 23.)

Heavenly Father,

You want me to be like your son, Jesus. That means living a life that is right and clean. I can't do this without your help. I get mixed up with the wrong people and sometimes make some silly choices and mistakes. I want to stay on the right path and follow you as you lead me in your ways. Help me to choose my friends carefully and to think twice about who I allow to have a say in my life. In all things help me to look to you as my Good Shepherd leading me into the best life possible. Amen.

19

The Whirlwind and the Rain

IN a tiny one-roomed house covered by straw thatch lived a poor widow seventy years old. Unfortunately the thatch was so badly in need of repair that whenever the rain and wind came the roof leaked, and the framework of the cottage shook. At last one of the beams which fitted into another became disjointed and threatened the collapse of the house.

This Chinese woman had not been a Christian long, but she knew that prayer works, and she also knew that she could talk to her Heavenly Father about everything. Often she would remind Him that she was a poor woman with no money to buy new straw for the thatch, nor could she afford to pay for repairs to the beam, and she would ask Him to look after her tumbling-to-pieces-little-house. One day when dark clouds were gathering for a great storm, her only son, who still worshipped idols, rushed in saying, "Mother, burn incense to the idols, or tonight the house will be destroyed." But she knew a better way, and kneeling down repeated the familiar prayer: "Heavenly Father, You know I am a poor widow and have no money to call a carpenter to mend that beam, and I have no way of getting new straw to patch the roof either; please look after my little house."

While still on her knees, the rain fell in bucketfuls and a whirlwind shook the little house violently. The son was terrified and shouted, "Mother, get up and burn incense; get up quickly

and burn incense," but she continued, "Heavenly Father, You know all about that loose beam and my poor roof. You look after it, please." After the hurricane had ceased she rose from her knees and looked up to find that the violent shaking had brought the ends of the two beams tightly into place again! "Thank You, Heavenly Father," she said, "You knew all about it, and so You just mended it."

All that night the rain continued, but not a drop came through the thatched roof. This was so remarkable that early the next morning the old woman went out to investigate. To her joy and amazement she saw patches of new straw on the roof: the wind had blown it on to her roof from the neighbours' stacks, and the heavy rain had patted it into the holes as if a human hand had done the work! "Thank You, Heavenly Father," again and again she said, "You knew all about it, and so You just blew the straw over and mended it for me."

What about me?

"And when you pray, do not keep on babbling like pagans, for they think they will be heard because of their many words. Do not be like them, for your Father knows what you need before you ask Him" (Matthew 6:7-8).

I have to admit that sometimes it is hard to trust in somebody that I cannot see. When I pray I can feel like I'm just talking to the air, and I feel like I have to make sure that God somehow hears me. Do I ever think about how near He is to me all the time? Have I really understood that He already knows everything that is going on in my life, even before I talk about it when I pray? Do I sometimes try to come up with ways that I think will help God to hear my prayers—saying it enough times, yelling it loud enough? Do I understand that He already knows my needs and is more than willing to help me in everything I face? (For further study you can read Psalm 139.)

Heavenly Father,
You know more about me than I can ever understand. You even know how many hairs are on my head. And you still love me and want to work in my life as I bring my problems and needs to you. Help me to understand that there is nothing in my life or my heart that you do not know about. You know everything and can fix everything. Help me to trust you to answer when I pray. Amen.

Pioneers All

A pioneer is one "who goes before to prepare the way for others." On opening up a huge country like China to the Gospel there was scope for pioneers of all kinds. I will tell you of five of them.

(20)

Francis Xavier

IF you are sitting beside the driver of a car, you may have noticed that he has what are called a starter and an accelerator. With the first he starts his engine, and with the second he speeds up his car. They do not do the main work, but they are most important parts of the machine. There are some people whose chief job seems to be to get other folk started on something, or to stir them on to work harder. Francis Xavier was like that. He was a great missionary, but all his own work in the mission field was limited to ten years. It was not the amount of work that he did that counted, but his zeal which set on fire the devotion of other people.

Little Francis was born in 1506 in a castle in the Basque country of Spain. Some of the world's greatest men were born about that time too—Shakespeare, Luther, John Knox, Tyndale the Bible translator, and the famous Admiral Drake. Francis had five older brothers, and some of them were soldiers; but Francis was a student, and when he was a tall athletic lad of nineteen he galloped off on horseback to the University of Paris. Here he worked hard, getting up at four in the morning to be at lectures by five! He was a Roman Catholic and heard the call to be a missionary, and indeed, became a great one.

The Basque people are ardent and enthusiastic by nature, and Xavier certainly was; when he loved, he loved passionately.

After his conversion Francis wanted to do nothing but preach Christ to those who did not know Him. Once in a dream he could not help calling out to God, asking for more to do.

At the end of a long and perilous journey he reached India in May, 1542. He was a born pioneer, and though he found doors shut on every hand, he kept saying, "I must open up a way." That was the key of Xavier's life. He was always pushing at closed doors. With a little bell in his hand he would walk up and down the streets inviting people to come and hear about Jesus Christ. But he was not satisfied with working in India only. Hearing that a ship was sailing east, he went on board it in April, 1549, and set out for Japan. Writing home he said, "God our Lord has power over the tempests of the Chinese and Japanese seas, which are the greatest known, and has control over all the sea robbers. I fear nought but God, lest He chastise me for being slack in His service, and useless for the advancement of the Name of Jesus Christ."

After about two and a half years in Japan, Xavier greatly desired to open up work in China. This was a more difficult task, but nothing would daunt him. He was ready to lay down his life for the Lord Jesus, and so he did, for he died within sight of China on an island now called St. John. Among some of the last words Xavier wrote were, "You may be very sure of one thing: the devil will be tremendously sorry to see the Company of the Name of Jesus enter China; but you may be sure of this too, that with God's help and favour I will confound the devil here."

He did not enter China, but his zeal has moved many others to do so. The unquenchable love and devotion of men like Francis Xavier have borne much fruit.

A Spanish Castle of the 16th Century

What about me?

"I have fought the good fight, I have finished the race, I have kept the faith. Now there is in store for me the crown of righteousness, which the Lord, the righteous Judge, will award to me on that day—and not only to me, but also to all who have longed for his appearing" (2 Timothy 4:7-8).

Francis Xavier, like the apostle Paul, was faithful to God's call on his life until his very last breath. He was willing to give up many things, go to unknown lands, and face many dangers—so that people could hear about Jesus Christ in lands that had never before heard of Him. What have I ever given up for Jesus Christ? Where would I be willing to go? What would I be willing to do? Do I think about what God might want me to do with my life? (For further study you can read 2 Kings 22:1-20; 23:1-28.)

Heavenly Father,
Even though you are mighty and all-powerful, you choose to use people to do your work. You ask people to follow you and to live their lives for your glory. I am not sure what I could do, but I want to be a person who is willing to do your work whatever it might be. Help me to learn to listen to your voice and to be willing to do what you ask me, now and later on in my life. Amen.

(21)

Robert Morrison

TWO hundred and fifty-five years after Francis Xavier had died within sight of China, Robert Morrison, the first Protestant missionary to that great country, landed at Canton. Both were pioneers, but they were very different men. Xavier was a Roman Catholic, Morrison a Protestant. Xavier was a Spaniard, hasty and ardent. Morrison was—well, what was he? For the moment we will call him British, and discuss his country later. He was far from hasty like Xavier; he was one of that dogged type of which it is said, "It's dogged that does it." And he needed to be a dogged man, for he had a tough task. If there is one lesson more than another that his life teaches, it is the lesson of quiet, steady determination which refuses to be beaten. There were many more brilliant men, but none more determined not to look back after he had put his hand to the plough.

We have called Robert Morrison British because the Scots say he was Scottish, and the English contend that he was an Englishman. His father was a Scot who left the land of his birth and came south seeking work. He settled as a farm labourer in the border country between the Tweed and the Tyne, and there fell in love with a Northumbrian girl who became his wife. Robert was their youngest son, and so you shall decide whether he was Scottish or English.

As a boy he worked hard at making clogs. His uncle was a patten-ring maker, that is, a maker of the iron ring worn under the wooden clog to keep it from the wet. Though young Robert worked from six in the morning until eight at night, he never became very good at this work. He certainly worked hard and also studied hard, teaching himself shorthand, Latin, and other subjects. While quite young he had the desire to be a missionary and wrote, "My desire is, O Lord, to engage where labourers are most wanted. Perhaps one part of the field is more difficult than another. I am equally unfit for any, but through Thy strength I can do all things." This was the man for a tough job, and Morrison got it.

It is not easy today to realise how difficult his task was. It was decided to send him to China to translate the Bible into Chinese. Most men said it could not be done, and the great East India Company, who were in command of all the ships and trade in the Far East, said that no missionary should go to China. There were no books to help him learn the language. There was no dictionary, and the Chinese Government said that if any Chinese scholar taught a foreigner the language, he should have his head cut off!

As no English ship would take him, he sailed for America, determined to go in an American ship to Canton. When he was buying his ticket in America, the shipowner turned to him and, with an unkind smile, said, "And so, Mr. Morrison, you really expect that you will make an impression on the idolatry of the great Chinese Empire?" "No, sir," said Morrison, "I expect God will."

So Morrison sailed in an American ship, reaching Canton after a seven months' voyage, and he lived with an American merchant in Canton—the only city where foreigners were allowed to live in those days. If he had not had this American friend, he would have been sent home by the British merchants. In a bare room, with a big Bible commentary to shield his candle from the wind, he worked late night after night studying Chinese. He made a dictionary, though it took him years to do. He translated the Bible, almost unaided, though that took him twelve long years to finish. He was often in fear of life being taken; the Chinese who helped him were hunted from place to place and sometimes thrown into prison. His type was seized and destroyed; his paper was burned, but as we said at the beginning, "It's dogged that does it." Morrison lived to finish his task and to welcome other missionaries to China.

In twenty-seven years he only had one furlough, and during that time King George IV, who was then King of England, sent for him and congratulated him. But what rejoiced Morrison more than going to the Palace, was that he had begun a work which was to continue, and is still going on. What strides have been made since Morrison was the brave, lonely pioneer in Canton!

What about me?

"Like the coolness of snow at harvest time is a faithful messenger to those who send him; he refreshes the spirit of his masters" (Proverbs 25:13).

Robert Morrison had amazing courage and would not give up! To keep going in hard times, just so that people would have the Bible in their own language was a wonderful commitment to God. Do I know anybody that has never seen a Bible? Do I understand that God often uses people who are not necessarily "superheroes"? Have I learned what it means to give myself completely to God? If not, how can I find out? Am I ready to do whatever God might ask me? If I am willing, He can make me able and prepared. (For further study you can read Jeremiah 1:4-10.)

Heavenly Father,

I am not anybody special, but I am learning what it means to be faithful to you and your call. Please help me to be willing to be whatever you need me to be in order to do what you want in my life. Help me remember that, even though I often feel like I am too weak, it is at those times that you show how strong you really are. Amen.

Adam Dorward

"Beat the foreigner! We already have three religions, we will not have a fourth." So said the men of Hunan, the most determined of all China's peoples. Some townsfolk collected money with which to buy swords, knives, flags, and uniforms for the purpose of resisting any attempt the foreign missionaries might make to gain a foothold in their province.

It was as a pioneer to these determined powerful people that Adam Dorward went. Few pioneers have tackled a tougher task, and though he did not live to see Hunan opened to the Gospel, he did more than any other man to prepare the way.

Adam Dorward was born just across the border in Scotland, and had in him the sturdy indomitable spirit of the men of the Border. He had a comfortable home in Galashiels, and all the promise of a prosperous career before him, for he was taken into partnership with his uncles in a business for weaving Scotch tweeds. But hearing the call of God to go to China, he gave up business to prepare for missionary work, and sailed with Mr. Hudson Taylor in 1878.

Adam Dorward's ambition was to be a pioneer in Tibet. The harder and rougher the task, the more it appealed to him. Tibet was needy, to enter it almost impossible, therefore he wanted to try. But, instead, he was appointed to work in the province of Hunan. He was not at all disappointed, indeed he was glad,

because in some ways Hunan was more needy than Tibet. It is bigger than the whole of England, with about twenty million people in it. It lies right in the heart of China, and was to China something like a citadel is to a castle. The Hunanese had sworn that the foreigner and his Gospel should have no place in their province whatever.

For eight years Dorward travelled and worked without finding even a tiny room he could call a home. He visited nearly every city in the province, and suffered great hardships and insults without complaint. One day he had his head badly cut open by a brick that was thrown at him, but all he said was, "I want to glorify God even in such experiences as this." Hardship was all part of the day's work for him as Christ's soldier.

Adam Dorward never spared himself. Once while he was ill, a message came from another sick missionary asking help. Instead of nursing himself, Dorward took a long and difficult journey to reach his missionary friend. But it was too much for him in his own ill health, and he died. He gave his life for Hunan and for his brother missionary. In one of his letters he wrote, "I

117

have at all times the knowledge that God is with me. I want my body, heart, and mind to be entirely consecrated to God and used in His service."

One great lesson to be learned from Adam Dorward's life is that we must not judge missionary work by visible results. Dorward lived, worked, and died without the joy of seeing any results. God the great husbandman calls some men to plough, that is to open up places for the Gospel; and some to sow the Good Seed; and others to reap, that is to see people accepting Jesus Christ as Saviour. Since Dorward's day many people in Hunan province have turned from worshipping idols to trust in God, but it was this brave pioneer's faith and courage that opened up the way for them to do this.

What about me?

"Then I heard the voice of the Lord saying, 'Whom shall I send? And who will go for us?' And I said, 'Here am I. Send me!'" (Isaiah 6:8).

Pioneers do some pretty incredible things. They take chances and do hard things that those who follow after them will never have to do. Sometimes they never even see anything happen after all their hard, hard work. Do I ever think about some of God's pioneers—those found in the Bible or in church history books? Do I think about how they lived and the example they set for people of my time? What can I learn from their lives? Am I willing to follow in their footsteps? (For further study you can read Hebrews 12:1-3.)

Heavenly Father,

Pioneers are special people. Jesus himself was a pioneer. Help me to think about the men and women who were willing to take great chances for you. Please put that same strength in me and help me to be willing to be one who will go if you ever ask me to. Help me remember to pray for those who are pioneers in different parts of the world right now, working for your kingdom and your glory. Amen.

(23)

Harold Schofield

When Harold Schofield went to China as a medical missionary many of his friends said he was mad. "Just fancy," they said, "a man with such a brain and such good prospects going abroad to work among the Chinese! Why, he might do anything he liked in this country; he could make a fortune; he could get a great name for himself and become the pride of his profession. He *must* be mad to throw away such possibilities!"

Robert Harold Schofield was born in London in 1851, two years before Hudson Taylor sailed for China. As a boy he was full of fun and ready for any prank. At one time his parents lived in a house with a thatched roof, and he and his brother Alfred, who also became a distinguished doctor, used to go up on the roof and, on a wet board, toboggan down from the ridge to the gutter, never realising the danger that they might be shot over the edge into the yard below. What holidays those two brothers had together! Once they travelled from the north of England, a distance of five hundred miles by water, along the rivers Mersey, Severn, and Thames to London Bridge. They only had a small boat for this long journey, and then they wrote a book called *The Waterway to London*. On another holiday they were nearly drowned in one of the Irish lakes when their boat capsized two miles from the shore.

But it was not all play with Harold Schofield. At school he took all the prizes, and at college it was just the same. It would take a page to tell of all the examinations he passed and of all the scholarships and honours he gained. At Manchester, Oxford, and London Universities, and at St. Bartholomew's Hospital, he carried all before him—Greek Testament prizes as well as medical honours. Degrees and honours were showered upon him in each University. But he remained the most humble of men. After his death when a box in which he kept his numerous diplomas and over forty certificates was opened, they found a slip of paper on which he had written: "God resisteth the proud, but giveth grace to the humble."

One day while he was a medical student he took up the *Life of Dr. Elmslie,* who had been a medical missionary in Kashmir. The reading of that book made him resolve to place his life and gifts at the feet of Jesus Christ and be a medical missionary also. So in 1880, crowned with medical honours, he sailed for China as a member of the China Inland Mission, to become a pioneer missionary doctor in the northern province of Shansi. He settled in the capital, the great city of Taiyuan, with its massive walls eight miles round and many battlemented gates. Little did he know that just twenty years later this city was to become famous, or shall we say infamous, by the murder of forty-four missionaries and children, and a great number of brave Chinese Christians. Here it was that Dr. Schofield opened the first missionary hospital in that vast province, which is larger than Scotland and Ireland put together.

The claims upon a medical man's days are so many that it is especially difficult for him to find time really to master the Chinese language, but Dr. Schofield determined not to play at Chinese, as he said, so he set to work in earnest. Even when he went for a walk, he was studying the Chinese street signs, and he wrote up his diary in Chinese characters! To speak Chinese

1851 — 1883

HAROLD SCHOFIELD

is difficult enough, but it is much harder to write it. He was not satisfied with merely healing the sick who came to his hospital; he would sit by their bedside and talk to them about their farms, their crops, their trades, their friends, in fact about almost anything that would give a friendly feeling, so that he might introduce Jesus Christ and His Gospel to them.

And now comes something we find hard to understand. Within three years he died from typhus fever contracted from a patient. How strange it seems that after all those years of study he should only be spared to work for three years in China! To us it looks as though all his gifts and all his valuable knowledge had been thrown away. But just before he died he asked his friends to tell Mr. Hudson Taylor that those three years had been the happiest of his life, and then he repeated these lines:

A little while for winning souls to Jesus,
Ere we behold His beauty face to face;
A little while for healing soul diseases,
By telling others of a Saviour's grace.

It all seems very sad and mysterious, but we must remember that Jesus Christ was crucified after only three years' work as a great missionary to this poor world. So we must not measure God's time by years, but by love and obedience. It is these things that make a short time precious. A little gold is worth much more than a small mountain of copper. The little seed sown in the ground brings a great harvest. So it has proved to be in Dr. Schofield's case. Later, a large hospital was built at Taiyuan by the Baptist Missionary Society, and no one can say how many have been healed and helped and turned to God there through all the skill and love shown to them.

What about me?

"But whatever was to my profit I now consider loss for the sake of Christ. What is more, I consider everything a loss compared to the surpassing greatness of knowing Christ Jesus my Lord, for whose sake I have lost all things. I consider them rubbish that I may gain Christ..." (Philippians 3:7-8).

There are many people who have given up a lot to serve Jesus Christ in some special way. Other people often thought they were crazy and doing the wrong thing, still they wanted to follow Jesus more than anything in the world. How wonderful knowing Jesus in that way must be! How do I think of Jesus and the other things that are important in my life? Is He more important than all the rest? What would I give up in order to follow Him? What does Jesus promise if we do? (For further study you can read Matthew 19:16-30.)

Heavenly Father,
You have already given up the greatest thing when you sent us your son. Nothing I could do would be as good as that, but I want to be sure that I am willing to give up anything that would stand in the way of knowing you or obeying you. Help me to always keep my eyes on you and to remember that all the things from this world will pass away one day. Only you and what we do for you will last forever. Amen.

24

F. W. Baller

F. W. BALLER was one of the best known missionaries in China. Brimful of energy, doing nothing by halves, he was yet full of fun and humour. He was a born mimic and would have made a good actor. He could imitate any sound, from a baby crying to the rattle of an anchor's chain as it plunged into the sea.

This great gift of imitation made him a fine linguist, for he could copy like a parrot any dialect he heard spoken. He could sit with half a dozen Chinese from different parts of China and speak to each one in turn in his own dialect. To his listeners this was nothing short of marvellous.

Frederick William, more usually known as "F.W.", Baller was born in 1852, the year before Hudson Taylor first sailed for China. As a young man he was a carpenter, as his father had been before him. As you might expect, he was full of spirit and life, and a ringleader in all kinds of harmless mischief. As a boy he was expelled from Sunday School because he couldn't keep in all his fun and jokes. When he was offered a Bible he refused it; but he had a good mother whose influence never left him. As he grew up he joined one of the Thames Rowing Clubs, and it was his aim to become the champion sculler of England! He used to spend his Sundays on the river, but one day he had a shock which led to his conversion. He was due to row for his boat, but feeling unwell one Sunday, he asked a friend to take

his place. It so happened that that boat sank and his friend was drowned. This shook him, for he thought how easily it might have been he himself that met with the accident, and this led to his turning to God.

From this time he was just as keen for God as he had previously been eager for pleasure. When he was handing out tracts one day on the Thames Embankment, he saw some of his old rowing friends coming towards him. He was tempted to slip up a side street, but overcoming his cowardice he went to them and spoke a word for his Master. In later life he always felt that that had been a most important action, and he always thanked God that He had given him courage to conquer and not be ashamed of being known as a Christian.

When he was nineteen he heard God's call to China, and after nearly two years of training he sailed for that distant land when he was a few months short of his twenty-first birthday. Starting so young to master a new language, and having natural gifts that way, he soon became as much at home in Chinese as if he had been born in that country.

We have classed Mr. Baller among the pioneers, for he not only did tough pioneer journeys in hostile Hunan province, and worked unstintingly amongst starving famine refugees in north China, but he was a literary pioneer too. As you can imagine, he developed into a quite unusually gifted Chinese scholar, not only as regards spoken Chinese, but he so mastered the strokes and style of brush-pen Chinese, that he was given the title of "Master of the Pen." He prepared primers, dictionaries, and many other helps for those embarking on learning Chinese. A copy of his primer and Baller's Dictionary had a place on the study table of the last Emperor of China in the Palace in Peking. Besides writing smaller books Mr. Baller gave years of work in connection with the committee on revising the whole Bible in Chinese.

His last work was a *Life of Hudson Taylor*, which he wrote entirely in Chinese character by himself, when he was seventy years old and far from well. The first finished, printed copy of this book was put into Mr. Baller's hands just the day before he died. It was a fitting close to a busy gifted life—finishing the work God had given him to do.

What about me?

"I have brought you glory on earth by completing the work you gave me to do. And now, Father, glorify me in your presence with the glory I had with you before the world began" (John 17:4-5).

It is important that we finish jobs that we are given to do. This teaches us what it means to be faithful. Nobody has ever been more faithful to the task He was given than Jesus himself. He was sent on the greatest mission of all, and He finished the work He was given to do. Do I ever think that God may have something for me to do? Do I ever think what His plan for me might be? Am I aware that doing what He asks me is the best way to show that He is working in my life? (For further study you can read the book of Nehemiah.)

Heavenly Father,

You have a great plan for each person's life. You make each one of us. Help me to know that you have a plan for my life too. I want to be like Jesus and do whatever you ask me to do—now and later in my life. Help me to learn what it means to be true to you and to please you by doing each thing that you ask me to do. Amen.

Buy online at our website: **www.KingsleyPress.com**
Also available as an eBook for Kindle, Nook and iBooks.

The full "Pirate Ship" story can be read in *A Present Help* by Marie Monsen, published by Kingsley Press.

A Present Help
By Marie Monsen

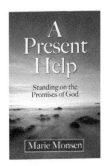

Does your faith in the God of the impossible need reviving? Do you think that stories of walls of fire and hosts of guardian angels protecting God's children are only for Bible times? Then you should read the amazing accounts in this book of how God and His unseen armies protected and guided Marie Monsen, a Norwegian missionary to China, as she traveled through bandit-ridden territory spreading the Gospel of Jesus Christ and standing on the promises of God. You will be amazed as she tells of an invading army of looters who ravaged a whole city, yet were not allowed to come near her mission compound because of angels standing sentry over it. Your heart will thrill as she tells of being held captive on a ship for twenty-three days by pirates whom God did not allow to harm her, but instead were compelled to listen to her message of a loving Savior who died for their sin. As you read the many stories in this small volume your faith will be strengthened by the realization that our God is a living God who can still bring protection and peace in the midst of the storms of distress, confusion and terror—a very present help in trouble.

Buy online at our website: **www.KingsleyPress.com**
Also available as an eBook for Kindle, Nook and iBooks.

THE AWAKENING

By Marie Monsen

REVIVAL! It was a long time coming. For twenty long years Marie Monsen prayed for revival in China. She had heard reports of how God's Spirit was being poured out in abundance in other countries, particularly in nearby Korea; so she began praying for funds to be able to travel there in order to bring back some of the glowing coals to her own mission field. But that was not God's way. The still, small voice of God seemed to whisper, "What is happening in Korea can happen in China if you will pay the price in prayer." Marie Monsen took up the challenge and gave her solemn promise: "Then I will pray until I receive."

The Awakening is Miss Monsen's own vivid account of the revival that came in answer to prayer. Leslie Lyall calls her the "pioneer" of the revival movement—the handmaiden upon whom the Spirit was first poured out. He writes: "Her surgical skill in exposing the sins hidden within the Church and lurking behind the smiling exterior of many a trusted Christian—even many a trusted Christian leader—and her quiet insistence on a clear-cut experience of the new birth set the pattern for others to follow."

The emphasis in these pages is on the place given to prayer both before and during the revival, as well as on the necessity of self-emptying, confession, and repentance in order to make way for the infilling of the Spirit.

One of the best ways to stir ourselves up to pray for revival in our own generation is to read the accounts of past awakenings, such as those found in the pages of this book. Surely God is looking for those in every generation who will solemnly take up the challenge and say, with Marie Monsen, "I will pray until I receive."

Buy online at our website: **www.KingsleyPress.com**
Also available as an eBook for Kindle, Nook and iBooks.

Other Books for Children

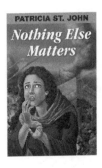

Nothing Else Matters

A powerful and moving story based on real events in the bitter conflict in Lebanon. Lamia and her family are caught up in the fighting, with tragic consequences. Lamia struggles with the hatred that threatens to destroy her, until she grasps that forgiveness and love are the most important things. Nothing else matters.

The Victor

Philo, a fisherman's son, lives in Phoenicia in the first century. Evil hangs over the family and it seems to come from his sister, Illyrica. Rumors reach Sidon of a prophet with amazing healing powers, but even the mention of His name has a disastrous effect. Philo runs away from home. Wherever he goes, he hears more news of this strange prophet known as the Victor. Who is He? what is He doing? What is the source of His Power?

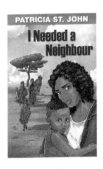

I Needed a Neighbour

The refugee camp is crowed with sick and starving people. Two new arrivals, a teenage girl, Mehrit, carrying her little brother on her back, wait their turn patiently. What will happen to them? Will they ever find their parents again? A strong story of a family in a famine-stricken African country.

Made in the USA
Charleston, SC
14 June 2012